M000266242

TWILIGHT FOR THE GODS

Second Edition

TWILIGHT FOR THE GODS
THE ART AND HISTORY
OF FILM EDITING

By Jack Tucker, ACE
California State University – Long Beach

Bassim Hamadeh, CEO and Publisher
Carrie Montoya, Manager, Revisions and Author Care
Kaela Martin, Project Editor, Revisions
Chelsey Schmid, Production Editor
Jess Estrella, Senior Graphic Designer
Alexa Lucido, Licensing Supervisor
Natalie Piccotti, Director of Marketing
Kassie Graves, Vice President of Editorial
Jamie Giganti, Director of Academic Publishing

Copyright © 2019 by Cognella, Inc. All rights reserved. No part of this publication may be reprinted, reproduced, transmitted, or utilized in any form or by any electronic, mechanical, or other means, now known or hereafter invented, including photocopying, microfilming, and recording, or in any information retrieval system without the written permission of Cognella, Inc. For inquiries regarding permissions, translations, foreign rights, audio rights, and any other forms of reproduction, please contact the Cognella Licensing Department at rights@cognella.com.

Trademark Notice: Product or corporate names may be trademarks or registered trademarks, and are used only for identification and explanation without intent to infringe.

Cover images:
  Copyright © 2009 Depositphotos Inc./Pshenichka.
  Copyright © 2013 Depositphotos Inc./cokacoka.
  Copyright © 2012 Depositphotos Inc./dubassy.
  Copyright © 2011 Depositphotos/Kesu01.
  Copyright © 2013 Depositphotos/Andrey_Kuzmin.

Printed in the United States of America.

ISBN: 978-1-5165-1930-9 (pbk) / 978-1-5165-1931-6 (br)

*To Jackie Freeman
Who taught me video.
Rest in Peace.
You gave so much more than you got.*

Contents

Chapter

Twilight for the Gods

*I*t is twilight for the gods of time and space. They are fading away with the twentieth century. Their ability to take two unrelated shots and edit them together, creating a new relationship earned editors that name, and it is the basis of their art. Now electronic editing has erased the mysticism that long protected them and their craft. The editor's power over time and space is being usurped by the committee that sits behind him.

Electronics has opened the door to micromanagement. The editor is no longer alone with the film. Sitting behind him are the director, the producer, the executive producer, and the lead actor all eagerly helping him or her edit, and all covetous of the power of the gods. Collaborative art has gotten confused with mob rule.

When I interviewed Steve Cohen four years ago, he predicted that everyone would be an editor in the new world of electronics. It is happening sooner than he even imagined. The mysteries of the KEM and Moviola that baffled directors, producers, and teenage executives no longer guard the gate. Everyone is now computer literate, and the Avid is only a computer, so it naturally follows that everyone can edit. The noble six hundred editors of Hollywood in 1950 have been overwhelmed by the six million barbarians at the gate.

The ability to change images easily on a computer belies the art of editing. It is too easy. The mystery of the process of constructing scenes is gone, and there is no longer a need to think things out. Just try it. Like the infinite number of monkeys on the infinite number of typewriters creating the great novel, you'll hit the right arrangement of shots eventually. Editing by attrition. The committee will sort it out and vote on the result.

Gone is all thought of the years that talented editors spent learning and then honing their craft. The years of apprenticeship that nurtured Michael Kahn, Dede Allen, and Tom Rolf are unnecessary. Because the Avid does all the work, there is no need to get the best, most experienced person. Hire the cheapest. After all, how bad can it be?

Working on film, I had to make a commitment to my cuts. It took time and splicing tape to change them. I pre-edited my scenes in my mind while watching the dailies. Later, in the editing room, I honed at the bench the vision I had thought out. Sure, I reworked material, but there was thought behind it. Electronics requires no such commitment. It is "no-fault" editing.

Electronic editing is in many ways a godsend for film editing, but the downside is incompetence and indecision. Why is a system that claims to save time and money causing so much stress and overtime? Do we really need five versions of a scene? Must everything be rushed out without time for thought? Is not the time an artist spends alone with his soul what begets his best work?

I refuse to go quietly into the night. I did not spend thirty-five years at the bench to be a button-pusher. I will not be a party to committee editing. I love to collaborate with the director and even the producer at the proper times, but I do not need a dozen micromanagers sitting behind me while I edit. What I do need is respect for my craft and my skill and the time to make my magic.

We have to get beyond "committee editing" and go for the benefits of the electronic systems. The "liquid editing" that Orson Welles spoke of is here. But it needs to be in the hands of an experienced and talented film editor working alone with his material. The collaboration should consist not of orders fired over the editor's shoulder, but of discussions involving story, insight, vision, and inspiration from the filmmaker. This melding of talent produces brilliance.

Remember, the pendulum swings both ways. The art of editing will come again. We can bring it back with our personal commitment to it. The confusion and indecision that arrived with electronics will sort itself out. The gods of time and space aren't dead. They're only sleeping. A new dawn awaits.

KEEP THE FAITH

Editing is not a technical process.
It is an artistic process.
It is about storytelling.
What editors do is the final rewrite of the script.

—Jack Tucker, ACE

I wrote the editorial titled "Twilight for the Gods" in late 1999, when I was still editing the *Cinemeditor* magazine for the American Cinema Editors. It was an attempt on my part to discuss the effects of recent technological innovations on film editing. All through the 1990s, many a veteran film editor and assistant scrambled to become "technologically correct" by learning the latest digital editing system in a desperate attempt to hang on to their careers. Some successfully transitioned into the new world of the twenty-first century, and some simply walked away from changes they were not comfortable with.

I was fortunate to have the opportunity to work with Avid, Lightworks, EMC2, D-Vision, MC Express, and even Final Cut Pro. Once I began to understand "digital thinking," I realized that these systems were all very similar. Digital editing made all things possible to a film editor. That editor was limited only by his or her imagination. But it was, as all technological advances are, a double-edged sword. Suddenly, there were unlimited choices, and everyone was an editor. Ease in making changes and the ability to save versions gave everyone a voice in how something was edited. What had once been a personal collaboration between director and editor was open to the committee.

Editing is the one single thing that makes motion pictures an art form. Without it, you are simply recording an event, either real or staged. But the ability to alter time and space elevates that recording process to an art form. That is why editors are called the gods of time and space. The ability to speed up and slow down events and determine their order is why people are drawn to movies. To choose when to show something and for how long is a god-like power.

Editors are artists in much the same way that actors, directors, cinematographers, production designers, and so forth are. Almost everyone connected with the production of a film is an artist to some degree. Each individual's skills and experience shape the film. Artists bring inner truths to their work, and to do it properly, they need time alone with their material. I have always been able to sell this concept to the directors I have worked with. At the end of production I ask for two weeks to finish the editor's cut. After showing the director my version, I am willing to make any changes the director wants. I welcome the collaboration with another artist to achieve the best possible version of the film.

Back in the 1990s, I edited a little feature called *The Double 0 Kid*. It was about a teenage James Bond and was directed by Duncan McLaughlin. Duncan had been an editor in South Africa, and I was eager to collaborate with him on the cut. After running the first cut, which the producer described as "the best first cut I have ever seen," we retired to the cutting room to begin the director's cut.

We worked in a unique manner. I would run a scene on the KEM with Duncan. He would say, "That's good, but I see how to make it better." Because Duncan was an editor, I would leave the cutting room and wander about the Paramount lot, where we were renting space. After a time I would return and see what had been done. Then I would say, "That's great, but let me try something." Duncan would go off, and I would improve on his work. In this manner we kept "one-upping" each other. In the end we came up with a cut that was better than what either of us would have achieved on our own.

Now, I'm not one for recommending that directors cut their own films. As a rule, I say that the director who cuts his own film is like the lawyer who defends himself. He has a fool for a client. In the case of *The Double 0 Kid*, I was working with an established editor, and we were both working from my editor's cut. There are, of course, notable exceptions, Charlie Chaplin being one. The real problem with a director cutting his own film is that when he sits down to edit, he becomes an editor, and we have lost the film's director. A film needs a director to guide the assembled artists on both sides of the camera.

I had the good fortune of becoming acquainted with director Robert Wise (*The Sound of Music, The Sand Pebbles, West Side Story*), who had begun his career as an editor. He edited *Citizen Kane*. I asked him if Orson Welles had spent much time in the cutting room with him. Wise replied, "He never came into the cutting room. Didn't even know where it was. He watched cut footage in the theater, like all directors did in those days."

Welles would watch the cut scenes in a screening room and give notes to Wise. This was common practice in the 1940s. It had two great advantages. Number one, Welles was always the audience. He never got into the minutiae of the cutting room. Each time he saw a scene, he was unencumbered by how it was assembled. It either worked or it didn't. Number two was that Robert Wise was free to try all manner of things without Welles hanging over his shoulder. He could really make cuts that might turn out to look stupid, with no one to witness it.

This method of editing was used by Gerry Hambling, ACE, and Alan Parker in their many collaborations. Parker could come into the cutting room and discuss scenes with Hambling all he wanted, and even run cuts and alternate takes. But the moment Gerry reached for his splicer, Parker had to leave. As Hambling explained, "If you're in the room, I'm going to be trying to please you, and I won't be free to try other things."

When director John Huston was looking at a cut of *Moby Dick* with editor Russell Lloyd, they discussed making a slight change. Russell suggested that Huston come up to the cutting room while he made the change and approve it on the Moviola so that they wouldn't have to run the change. Huston was horrified. "That would be like watching my wife getting dressed. I just want the end result." Huston never came to the cutting room.

Over the years, the situation has changed. Newer directors coming out of film school are anxious to be part of the editing process. They have not experienced the factory-like studio system, where editing was more in the studio's hands than the director's. When I worked for Eric Bercovici at MGM on the television series *Jessie*, he did not see the point of his directors having a cut. His theory was this: "I'm the executive producer, and I have final cut. The editors know how I want things, so a director's cut is a waste of time. They should be out looking for their next job." This didn't sit well with the DGA, but we editors were not members of that guild.

I am willing to work with a director in any fashion he chooses, but I still like to do the first cut by myself. This is not always possible. When I worked as an additional editor for my former assistant, Michael Knue, ACE, on *Nightmare on Elm Street IV*, we were under a drastic time crunch to get the picture out. Director Rene Harlan would come to the cutting rooms after shooting all day, and we would run cuts of the day's work for him. He would give his notes, and we would continue on. Despite the fact that four editors were cutting (and four units were also shooting), under Michael's leadership, the picture turned out rather well.

Since the time of my editorial, I resigned from *Cinemeditor* and have devoted myself to other pursuits. In 2000 I began teaching the art and history of film editing at California State University, Northridge, and in 2002 I began teaching media editing at California State University, Long Beach. I had previously lectured before various classes about editing and trained many assistants, but I had never taught a full course. To prepare myself for this class, I began searching for a textbook to use with my lectures. Though there are many useful books on the subject of film editing, I had difficulty in finding one that addressed how editing developed and its relationship to technology.

I began researching the origins of editing and quickly realized how much it was tied to technological advancements. Before 1923, there was no real editing machine. Cuts were made without the benefit of work print, and although negative was run through projectors, the results were evident only after a reel was printed. The people who cut the picture together were called "patchers," because they literally cut the negative pieces and then glued them together. When the Moviola came along, patchers were now able to become editors. About this time it was decided to make a print from the negative to protect it during the editing process. The editors could see what they were actually doing, and this opened up many new possibilities for how to edit a scene. When the KEM made its way into American filmmaking in the 1960s, with its ease in comparing performances, it further enhanced editing; and when the Avid and other digital systems appeared, the craft no longer had limits. To investigate the influence that technology has had on the art of film editing, and to guide students in mastering this craft, I decided to write this book.

I walked into my first editing room fifty years ago in December 1964. That was at Vandenberg Air Force Base in California. I, as a young airman, was assigned to the editorial department of the 1369th Photo Squadron at that location. The first editors I met were SSgt. Joseph Bettencourt, Airman Bob Jenkins, and a civilian employee, Oakley McGuire. These men were my introduction to the world of filmmaking, something I knew absolutely nothing about.

Because of my total ignorance of the film business, it was decided that I should apprentice for two months in the film lab before learning editing. I am grateful to whoever it was that made this decision, because it did give me a grounding for learning film editing. Immediately I found myself on the "dry end" of a 35 mm film processor. A film processing machine has two ends: the "wet" or dark end, where exposed film is loaded to be processed, and the "dry" or light end, where the now-processed film comes off. I worked the dry end, then graduated to film cleaning on the ultrasonic cleaner, and eventually ended up in positive assembly, where I learned to operate a pedestal hot splicer.

A year later, as the Vietnam War heated up, I was temporarily assigned to the Air Force's film studio in Hollywood, Lookout Mountain Air Force Station. There I was privileged to meet such legendary film editors as Les Milbrook, Donn Hayes (who gave

Figure 1.1. Film processing machine

the American Cinema Editors its name), William Holmes (who had won an Oscar for editing *Sergeant York*), and Chandler House. My association with these men forever changed my life and infected me with "the holy disease," the love of filmmaking—and particularly of film editing.

The Lookout Mountain editing department was reputed to have more than 450 years of experience among its members. They would often say, "We don't claim to know everything about film editing, but we did invent it." There was much truth to that remark. Some of them remembered when DeMille arrived, and all of them were products of their craft from the days of the silents.

From the beginnings of film, they had learned to tell stories with pictures. Without the aid of a soundtrack to explain things, they had learned to convey emotions, concepts, and ideas by arranging shots in a certain order. They learned to alter reality and create a new one. They could take two shots photographed years apart in different locations and put them together to create a scene that appeared real. This ability earned them and their peers the title "the gods of time and space." Even after the advent of sound, they remained visual artists, arranging their shots and using sound to enhance the effect.

My adoration of these men allowed me entry into their midst. I cleaned their splicers, blooped their tracks, rolled their trims, and spliced their cuts together. In those days, the Air Force had not converted to tape splicers, and the joining of shots was done on the large pedestal hot splicers by the assistants. Because I was eager to perform all these duties, my mentors began to pass on to me the wisdom of their craft. Bill Holmes

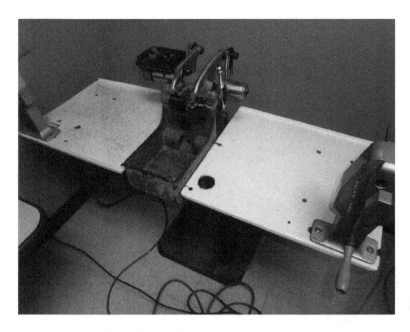

Figure 1.2. Pedestal hot splicer

taught me how to sync dailies, Les Milbrook gave me a chance to cut, and Chan House and Donn Hayes offered cutting advice.

Working with these men, I frequently heard stories of the old days. Eagerly I listened when two or more of them gathered to talk about how a famous film was cut and why certain things were done. I was taken under their collective wing and shown their secrets. Donn counseled, "Every cut should show something new to advance the story." Editing skills are acquired from contact with skilled editors. Any skills I have acquired began with these men.

They have all passed into editing history now. As I write this book, I wish I could still speak to them and ask them about how it all began. Over the years I have made the acquaintance of many editors: Tom Rolf, ACE; Dann Cahn, ACE; George Watters, ACE; Dede Allen, ACE; Peter Zinner, ACE; Michael Kahn, ACE; Donn Cambern, ACE; and Mark Goldblatt, ACE; to name only a few. Each of them has taught me about the craft. Some of them have shared stories and insights that I am going to share with you.

I realize that I am ill-equipped to completely cover the subject that I have set before me. I can contribute only what knowledge I have acquired over the years to the story of editing as I know it. Hopefully this will inspire other editors to write and add their pieces to fill in the gaps to form a complete history of our craft as well as an inspiration to future editors.

It is my hope that students who read this book will love the craft as I have and learn from it. It is magic, and we are the gods of time and space.

Chapter 2 *Inspiration*

I *nspired* means to be touched by the hand of God. In a broader sense, it means to connect to the Creator, the source of all natural phenomenon. All true art is the result of that connection, and I believe that all artists connect with the energy source that comes from the Creator when they are creating their art.

After you have been working in an art or craft for a while, you develop an inner sense of how to make things work. I make a few cuts in a sequence, and the material begins to take on a life of its own. My hands and mind work together, shaping the material into something new. The aim is to create a whole that is greater than the sum of the parts. That is what editing is all about. You take the performances the actors have given you with the intent of the writer and director and move them to a higher level.

To achieve this, you may labor for hours or even days. It is seductive and obsessive. As previously stated, editing is not a technical process. It is an artistic process. It is about storytelling. What editors do is the final rewrite of the script. Imagine a film cutting room at a studio sometime before the 1990s. Let's say MGM before it became Sony. It is twilight, and the sound of Moviolas can be heard in the early evening air as we stroll along Washington Row, the tiny cutting rooms that line the wall against Washington Boulevard. In the 1930s they had been dressing rooms. Jackie Cooper once told me that my cutting room had been his dressing room. "And I thought it was small when I was a kid," he said, surveying my work environment. Now they were cutting rooms for less prestigious projects. Pilots and features were cut in more spacious rooms throughout the lot, but when a pilot went to series, as a reward, the editors were condemned to Washington Row. The two floors of wooden rooms resembled a tenement in a New York slum. When I became associate producer on the *Jessie* television series, I searched in vain for better rooms for the editors. They only ones that I could find were reserved for Michael Landon and his *Highway to Heaven* editors. We ended up on Washington Row.

If you now imagine yourself walking along the Row, through each door can be seen the editors and their assistants working over benches and Moviolas, honing raw footage into finished films and television shows. The sound editors can be heard customizing sound effects for shows, while the ADR editors sync up the replacement dialogue that will seem like it was originally recorded that way. Music editors prepare their tracks for an upcoming mix.

If you stop at room 15, you will observe an editor at work. It is late. His assistant has departed for the day, and he works alone. He is intently reviewing a piece of film on his Moviola. Backward and forward he runs the machine, carefully studying the action embedded in it. His hands expertly guide the piece of film through the editing machine as he works.

Everywhere there is film in pieces about the room. Some is neatly filed in film racks. Some is hanging on the hooks of the trim bin, and some is haphazardly strewn across the floor, while still more is looped around the editor's neck like a celluloid serpent. As he works, he instinctively seems to be able to find the shots he is looking for.

The editor marks a frame with a white crayon that he holds in his right hand. He then slaps the piece onto the butt tape splicer on the bench and cuts off the marked piece. This trim he hangs on an appropriate pin in his film bin. The other piece remains on the butt splicer. He quickly searches for the next piece he is planning to cut to and views it on the Moviola. Back and forth he rolls it, until he locates the one perfect frame that will introduce the shot. He marks the frame before it and cuts it on the butt splicer. Then he joins it with tape to the previously selected shot.

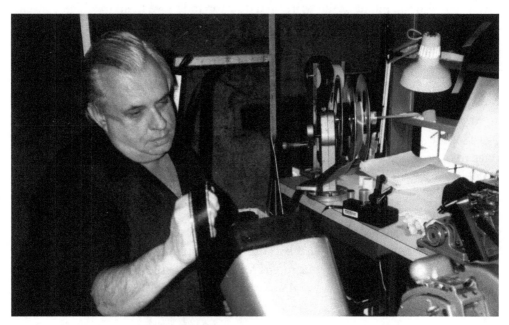

Figure 2.1. Editor working on Moviola

He places the two joined shots in the Moviola and views his cut back and forth. Now he has an opinion. Satisfied with his work, he prepares to move on. The phone rings. It is a foreign element amid the sounds of the editing room. At first the editor cannot identify the source of his interruption. He looks about the room. Finally, he focuses on the instrument on his bench and reaches for it.

"Hello," he answers to the person who speaks at the other end. It is a familiar voice.

"Oh, honey, it's you." He listens.

"Yes, dear, I'll be home shortly. Just a couple more cuts and I can stop for the night," he explains. "Not more than an hour. Then I'll be home for dinner. I promise. Two more cuts, and I'm out the door. … Yes. … Yes. … Love you."

He replaces the receiver and turns back to his task. He renews his promise to himself: "Only two more cuts." He inserts another shot into the Moviola and begins to examine it. Back and forth he runs it, until, at last, he settles on a frame. He marks it and joins it to the shots already cut, which are now being taken up on a Goldberg reel. He repeats this process with another shot, and then another and another.

The promise of a few minutes ago is quickly broken as each cut is made. Each cut suggests another, and the fever of creation moves through the editor. His hands fly to obey the images forming in his mind. Suddenly, he is outside of time as he sees the sequence flow together. As each cut suggests another, each idea inspires its fellow. The editor is alone with the film, and for this brief moment he is a god. He determines what will be seen and when. He totally controls time and space, and for this brief period the entire film is under his sole and complete control.

Outside, it has grown dark on Washington Row. The editor's fellows have left him, and the light shining from his room is the only beacon in this part of the sleeping studio. The guards make their rounds, checking doors and making sure all is secure. Some of them nod and say hello to the editor, but for the most part he is oblivious to them. He is alone with the film.

The editor works on through the night. He has almost no comprehension of the time and space around him. He is concerned only with the time and space of the film, which are firmly in his control. Like a sculptor searching for the statue in the marble, the editor hones and shapes the film to find the movie hidden in it.

There will never be another time like this first cut. It is a solitary moment between creator and creation. The editor knows that it is only his skill and instincts that are shaping the film at this point. It is a love affair, a first love, between editor and footage, with no outsiders involved.

When he runs the first cut, others will become involved, most notably the director. They will begin working together, and hopefully their collaboration will result in a good film that they both can be proud of. Together they will achieve something far greater than that which either would have achieved on his own. Sure, the producers and studio will have notes, but if the director and editor have collaborated correctly, these will merely be refinements.

The night air becomes cold, but the editor doesn't notice. As darkness approaches dawn, he is putting the final touches on the moment he has created out of the masses of film before him. The individual images have come together in a creation event that now has a life of its own. Eagerly he runs the entire cut sequence through the Moviola. A trim here, drop a shot here, move this shot over here, and the editor feels he has something that he can show. He has pulled life out of what was once only words on a page and independent strips of film.

Satisfied, he winds the sequence up on a reel and places it in a rack. He turns off the Moviola and the light over his bench. In the darkness the editor can see light coming from the east. As he walks out in front of Washington Row, he realizes that dawn is approaching and that he has worked through the night.

"My wife is going to be really pissed," he mumbles as he treads his way across the empty lot to the parking structure near Overland.

He tightens his jacket around him against the chilling dawn air. The studio he walks through is starting to come alive. The commissary is opening, and the backlot people are preparing for the day ahead. Stages are being unlocked, and crews are assembling to begin filming. The editor walks alone to his car. He will go home now for a few hours. He will attempt to save his marriage, catch a little sleep, and be back in the afternoon to continue the task of molding a cohesive movie out of separate shots.

Many more nights like this are to come before the film is finished. It is a struggle between editor and footage to find the picture and the dramatic flow that is hidden in the raw footage. In the end it will all come together and be over. The editor will move on to other projects, and the film will go out into the world to fulfill its destiny.

The events I have just described are in no way unique. This story could easily be called "A Day in the Life of a Film Editor." Many an editor, upon assuring his spouse that he would soon be home, has ended up lost in the creativity of what he was doing and arrived home several hours, or even days, later. A cut sequence, imagined in the screening room in a few minutes, can take hours to accomplish.

Editing is a seductive craft. It is reinforced learning. Every good cut leads you on to another cut, and every bad one leads you back to the bench to rework your idea. The god-like power of molding a visual story has a hypnotic, addictive effect that holds the editor in its grasp. It is a love affair between artist and film. Their coming together will be hot and passionate if their love is true. When it is through, they will part, as all lovers do when the affair is over and love has grown cold. Only the seeds of their passion will remain in the finished film as proof of their love.

The inspiration for this passion comes from somewhere. To be an editor, you need an epiphany that leads you to this work. For me it was James Dean in *East of Eden*. I had grown up watching Rock Hudson and Tony Curtis dashing about the screen, rescuing damsels and fighting the bad guys. That was the movie world for me. Every once in a while I saw something meaningful, such as *From Here to Eternity* or *On the Waterfront*, but mostly I saw more escapist entertainment. *East of Eden* was different.

Figure 2.2. You need an epiphany in EAST OF EDEN (1955), Warner Bros.

The creative use of Cinemascope and Dean shivering on top of the train so personalized his feelings and summed up the point of the film in this single shot. It is iconic and iconic shots are what movies are all about. The iconic shots will be remembered long after plot and story are forgotten.

I saw the film in 1960, after Dean had been dead for five years. I was sixteen, and, like many of my peers, I felt alone and unloved. James Dean's performance connected with me immediately. It touched my very soul. It was more than a movie. I was connecting with a piece of art for the first time. I knew at that point that I wanted to be part of filmmaking.

I was able over time to buy myself a cheap 8 mm projector and began collecting what films were available in that format. I even had a 8 mm print of *The Battleship Potemkin*. I also managed to buy an 8 mm camera. I began shooting monster movies with my friends. I purchased a set of cheap rewinds and a little viewer that I could hand-crank my film through. That was my introduction to editing. I would make my cuts and connect them with Mylar tape, using a product called a "quick splice."

My editing was very basic and not inspired. I was mainly joining together master shots and the occasional close-up that I would shoot for dramatic effect. I was inventing all over a craft that had already been invented.

Eventually I managed to buy a 16 mm Bell and Howell projector. I would rent films and show them in the basement to the neighborhood kids. When I entered college, I earned money as a projectionist in the Audiovisual Department. I learned splicing with a Griswold splicer and a razor blade. I wasn't very good at splicing. I didn't master that until I joined the Air Force and got into its filmmaking unit.

Chapter 3

The Basics

B asic editing consists of a series of rules that have been devised over the years by editors who came before us. Walter Murch, ACE (*Apocalypse Now*, *Cold Mountain*), has six rules for making a cut. Richard Halsey, ACE, (*Rocky*, *Edward Scissorhands*) has three basic rules for editing. For myself, it's all about story—telling a story in a coherent and interesting fashion.

Film editing is the pictorial version of writing. With writing you choose words and arrange them together in a coherent fashion to tell a story by creating images in the reader's mind. With film we select images, which are individual shots, and arrange them for the same purpose. If it is done properly, the viewer can follow what is happening and be interested in the story being told.

Richard Halsey's three rules are as follows: (1) use organization, (2) trust your instincts, and (3) always tell the truth. If you apply these rules in your editing, you should do well. The first rule, regarding organization, is all-important. An unorganized editing room is a disaster waiting to happen. There cannot be a lack of control in handling the footage.

I often say to my students, "At the set they create chaos. In the cutting room it is our job to bring organization to it." At the set they are shooting many different takes and many angles to capture a scene. When we receive it in Editorial, we must organize it so that we can produce the exact piece of a scene that we need, exactly when we need it. Fortunately, we have help at the set in doing this.

The script supervisor's job is to keep an exact accounting of everything that is shot and where it is intended to be in the script. These supervisors draw lines with a ruler indicating where each shot begins in the script and where it ends. They indicate what type of shot it is: a master, a three-shot, a two-shot, a single, an over-the-shoulder, or a tight close-up. The line indicates what dialogue and action is covered by the shot. If dialogue is off-camera, it is indicated by a squiggly line at the point of that dialogue.

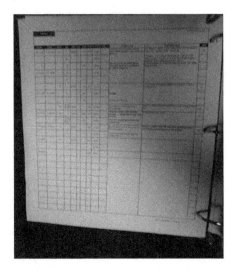
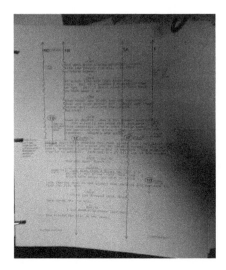

Figure 3.1. Shots described on the left-facing page are lined to the script on the right-facing page.

In addition to this, the script supervisor records information about the shot on the facing page. That is the page that is directly against the lined page. When both pages are open, the editor can see where the shot begins and ends and on the facing page read about the shot. On this page is recorded a description of the shot and how many takes were shot. Circles are used to indicate which takes the director prefers.

Figure 3.2. Camera reports

Also, the running time of the shot is indicated, plus which camera took it and the sound source.

The assistant cameraman and the sound recordist also keep records of what is shot. The Camera Report lists all the takes photographed on a particular roll of film. The sound man fills out a Sound Report with all sounds recorded on a particular tape. When I was on location I used to invite the script supervisor, the assistant cameraman and the sound man to my room for drinks and to go over their paper work. I wanted to make sure that we all agreed what was a circled take.

Circled takes are the ones that the director feels are what he wants printed to build the scene. When shooting on film, every take is recorded on the emulsion. We have to shoot each take, but we don't have to print them. Because of the cost of printing, takes considered not worthy are pulled from the negative after processing and set aside. They are called B negatives and are filed away. The good takes are printed and forwarded to the editor.

Sometimes the circled takes are not enough. Maybe something is missing. By looking in the lined script, the editor can see which B negative is available for the shot. The facing page has the running time of each take, and it is easy to see which takes are complete; they can be printed by indicating which camera roll and shooting date they are from. More than once a B negative has gotten me out of a tight spot.

In addition to the lined script and the facing page, the script supervisor produces a document known as the script supervisor's log. It has much the same information as the facing pages, but also it indicates call time, when the first shot was made, the lunch break, and the wrap time. A copy of it goes to the editor and also to the Production Department so that they can prepare their daily reports.

At the end of the day's shooting, all of this material must be copied and delivered. At the start of each day, the editing room needs the daily log, the facing pages, and the lined script. With this material it can be determined what has been covered and what

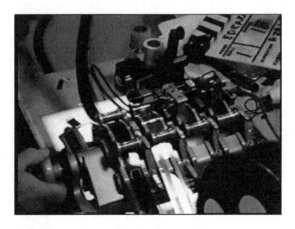

Figure 3.3. Picture and track synced

material will be coming to edit. These documents are essential when working on film to sync the picture and track together for viewing, coding, and preparing for editing. The documents are no less important when working digitally.

On film the dailies are synced by means of the clapper on the slate. The sound of the clapper is lined up with the first frame of the closed slate. The scene and take number is

Figure 3.4. Acme coding machine

indicated on the face of the slate and can be heard orally on the soundtrack. As sync is determined, each take rolls through the synchronizer until a roll of dailies is built. Each roll is a maximum of about nine hundred feet, or ten minutes, for ease in handling.

After syncing, each roll goes to coding. The separate picture and soundtrack have a common sync mark at their heads, which allows both rolls to be loaded onto a projector and play in sync. These head sync marks allow the picture and track to each be loaded separately onto an Acme coding machine, and matching codes can be laid down. These codes allow the picture and track to be lined up in sync. The codes also can be used as a filing system.

As scenes are synced and built into rolls, they receive a code number, which indicates what script scene they are part of. If the first scene was scene 8, take 1, the codes would begin with the prefix 008, indicating scene 8. Starting with the number 1,000, codes would go down every foot on the film and track. This would then be recorded into a code book. Scene 8, take 1 might be recorded as 008-1024 to 1136.

Alongside this in the code book are recorded the original film key numbers. These are numbers put on the original film as a latent image when the film is manufactured. The numbers appear when the negative is processed. They appear every foot and indicate what film stock the emulsion is and also are an arbitrary identification of the film frames. Camera rolls, lab rolls, and sound rolls are also indicated.

Renée DePalma's **THE SPY Code Sheet**

008-1000

Scene	Code #	Key #	Lab Roll	Camera Roll	Sound Roll	Description
8-3	1012-1044	KVO3 5744 4286-4235				Master
8-4	1045-1074	KVO3 5744 4239-4268				
8A-1	1075-1105	KV37 3104 2097-2127				
8S-1	1106-1191	KV37 5404 0420-0505		mos		
9B-5	1193-1234	KV37 5404 1173-1215				
8G	1233-1260	KV37 3254 1931-1957				
8G-2	1262-1345	KVO3 5744 5325-5358				
8G-3	1347-1467	KVO3 5744 5360-5479				
8E-1	1468-1520	KVO3 5744 4417-4470				
8F-2	1521-1593	KVO3 5744 4473-4544				

Figure 3.5. The code book: the film's database.

The code book is the Holy Bible in the cutting room. It is the database for the film, and with it shots can be located or identified. When I call out a code number to my assistant, he can easily find the pieces of film I need.

In the Moviola Editing System, after coding and viewing, the dailies for each shot are broken down individually and placed in a rack for the editor. Because of this, the system is nonlinear. It is the original nonlinear system. Shots are viewed on the

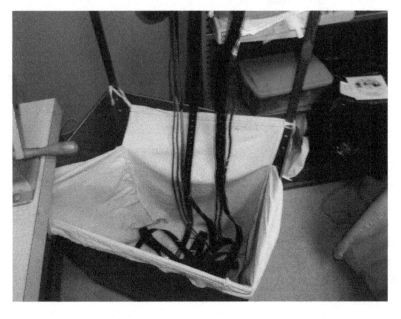

Figure 3.6. Trim bin

Moviola, and pieces are marked with an in and an out. They are then cut together and built through a synchronizer onto a reel. The head and tail trim is hung in a trim bin and eventually rolled up and filed by code number in a box.

If I want to lengthen a shot, I call out the code number, and my assistant should be able to place the trim in my hand in less than thirty seconds. If he can't, there is something wrong with the system, and I need a new assistant. Years ago, when I was cutting a film called *Illusions* for director Victor Kulle, I had Jennifer Dolce assisting me. We were so in sync as a team that I would start to ask for a trim as she was placing it in my hand. She watched what Victor and I were doing, and she was able to anticipate our needs. Victor said that he had never seen a cutting room so well organized.

Richard Halsey's second rule is to trust your instincts. This might also be described as knowing that your first instincts are the best. When I cut a scene, I have watched it in dailies. Usually by watching the dailies, particularly on the big screen, like God and DeMille intended, I have already cut the scene in my mind. In the cutting room, either on the Moviola or the Avid, it is merely a matter of implementing my vision. This may take several hours.

Usually I like to cut a scene in the afternoon and put it away when I go home at night. I try not to think about it again until the next morning when I take it out to look at it. At that time I make my final adjustments. Then I put it away until I assemble the first cut. As time goes on, we sometimes tend to second-guess ourselves. Then we make changes. I have found over time that this usually is a mistake.

Your first instincts tend to be correct. I was working with director Catherine Cyran on a scene from *The Prince and Me II: The Royal Wedding*. I don't remember exactly which scene, but we were having trouble with it. Finally Catherine said to me, "Show me your first cut of this. I think it was better." We were on an Avid, so, of course, all the cuts were preserved. I pulled up the cut, and we ran it. It was better. My first instincts had been correct. Catherine had me change it back.

Richard's third rule is the hardest: always tell the truth. When we are editing, we are searching for the truth. We are seeking the truth in an actor's performance, in the scene itself, and in the movie as a whole. That is the higher obligation we must serve. For a scene to work, it must be real, and it must speak the truth.

The stories we tell are mostly fantasies, made-up moments, but if they are made right, there is an element of truth in them. Even if you are editing *Godzilla Meets King Kong*, there needs to be truth. When it's real, it works.

Every experienced Editor knows that Editing is a search for the truth. I always thought this when I was totally unaware of Richard's rules. And I quickly learned that my first instincts were the best. Without organization we are totally lost.

Editing is divided into either dialogue scenes or action scenes. Most editors are stronger at one or the other, but one needs to be the master of both. In a dialogue scene, the lines propel the story forward, and drama is revealed by what a character says. The rhythms in this type of scene are crucial. How long to pause after each line? Where should we be? Seeing the person saying the line or the person reacting to it?

In the fall of 1980, after finishing work on the feature version of *Shogun*, I was able to secure the editing of the upcoming miniseries *The Winds of War*. It was being produced and directed by Dan Curtis for ABC-TV and Paramount Pictures Corporation. Bernard Gribble, ACE, a veteran of many Dan Curtis projects, had left while *Winds* was still in preproduction to take a feature, leaving a vacancy for an editor. I was excited to be involved in a project that, at the time, was the biggest miniseries ever attempted. We would be in production for more than a year.

I was on the picture for two years, and in the end five other editors joined me. For the first fourteen months I was the sole editor and managed to put more than half of the film in first cut. I edited battle scenes, love scenes, and dramatic moments, and much of this was done while Dan Curtis was half a world away. It was an exciting, creative time. Of the many sequences I cut, one stands out in its significance to film editing.

The sequence is early on in show five, titled "Of Love and War." The time is 1940; the place is London. England is at war with Germany, though America is still neutral. Pug Henry (Robert Mitchum), our main character, is a naval commander assigned as an attaché in Berlin, and is now temporarily visiting England to see how the British are holding up against the German bombings. He has become reacquainted with Pamela Tudsbury (Victoria Tennant), a woman half his age, while working at coordinating air defenses against the German aerial bombardments. They have been spending time together and are falling in love.

The scene opens in Pamela's apartment with the phone ringing. She eagerly answers, "Hello." Off camera is heard the voice of Pug Henry. He says, "Pamela?" She replies, "I'm so glad you called. In a quarter of an hour I would have been gone." So far all of this conversation is in the opening shot in her apartment.

At this point I make my first cut to Robert Mitchum sitting on a bed in his hotel room. He says, "Gone where?" and Victoria replies off camera, "I talked to Oxbridge. They're being very broad-minded. If I come back tonight, all is forgiven." Now I cut back to Victoria in her apartment, saying, "They're short-handed and expect heavy raids, so I must. I really must go back right away."

Now I cut back to Mitchum, and the dialogue continues. In all there are seventeen cuts in the sequence. Mitchum explains to Tennant that he has to return to Berlin and will be unable to see her again. She acknowledges that perhaps it is for the best, because she is engaged to a downed pilot and Mitchum is married. It is an emotional good-bye, with tears in Victoria Tennant's eyes by the end of the sequence.

As the talk becomes more emotional, I use tighter and tighter close-ups of the two actors. This is a very standard and correct way to edit this type of sequence, and it is quite effective in context of the story. The emotional truth in the scene plays quite well. But there is another element not apparent in the viewing of this sequence that

Figure 3.7. (A) (top) and 3.7 (B) (bottom) Synthesis of time and space. Robert Mitchum and Victoria Tennant shot one year apart in THE WINDS OF WAR (1983), Paramount Pictures.

illustrates the power of film editing. The two sides of the phone conversation were shot a full year apart, in radically different locales.

Robert Mitchum's side of the conversation was filmed in a practical location in downtown Los Angeles in December 1980. Victoria Tennant's side was filmed on stage 16 at Paramount Pictures in December 1981. Yet when the two sides are edited together, it gives the impression of an event actually happening continuously. Even when the mind knows these facts, it is fooled into believing the visual information it is seeing.

This altering of time and space by the editor is called the "synthesis of time and space." It is the single element that makes filmmaking an art form. Without it, you are merely recording an event, either real or staged. The ability to juggle time and space adds the dimension to filmmaking that elevates it to a true art form.

I could take this even further. I have several close-ups of Jeremy Kemp playing German General Von Roon, listening on a phone in another scene. If I added those close-ups into the scene with Pug and Pamela, I could create a whole other interpretation. Is General Von Room going to use the information he is hearing to blackmail Pug? The tender love scene could become one filled with intrigue and tension.

In 1998, *The Horse Whisperer* was released. It was directed by Robert Redford and edited by Tom Rolf, ACE. There is a key action sequence in the opening of the picture that demonstrates another important aspect of film editing. This is the accident sequence that sets up the plot. This sequence was edited several times by various people, including Rolf. The final version is the work of Hank Corwin, ACE.

The sequence opens with two young girls out riding horses in the snow. It intercuts with scenes of one girl's mother (Kristin Scott Thomas) at work, where she edits a magazine. Snow is falling in the foreground as the girls turn their horses off the road and start up a snowy slope. The next cut is back to the mother working with her associates on the magazine.

We cut back to the girls laughing and riding up the hill. The lead horse starts to slip on the slope. He loses his footing and slides back into the second horse, dislodging it. Soon both horses and riders are sliding back down the hill into the road. One girl's horse rights itself, while the other little girl lies unconscious on the road while her horse regains its footing. It starts dragging the little girl as her companion tries in vain to grab the reins and stop it.

At this point there is a cut to a large truck and trailer coming down the road. We cut back to the girls and back to the truck. Coming around a bend, the driver sees the girls in the road. Cut to his braking. The tail of the trailer swings out as he vainly tries to stop. Of course, he can't, and he strikes the girl being dragged and her horse.

This is a truly frightening sequence to see on a theater screen. The cuts beautifully build tension to the moment of impact, and many times I have seen viewers look away. The overwhelming emotional power of this moment is indescribable. The interesting thing about it is that it never happened.

Figure 3.8. Non-event: blue screen combines horse and truck in THE HORSE WHISPERER (1998), Touchstone Pictures.

It is a nonevent. The truck, the girls, and the horses never had this meeting. It is all suggested in the editing. Director Redford knew that this key sequence would have to be made in the editing room. The shots with the horse and the truck in the same frame are actually blue-screen composites. The accident was carefully staged in production and meticulously honed in editing to achieve the end result.

The scene is a marvelous example of editing at its best. It is a whole that is greater than the sum of the parts. The individual shots, great as they are, do not in any way reflect the power inherent in the correct arrangement of them. It is this arrangement that creates an emotional impact that far exceeds the impact of the individual shots.

This is the true power of editing. When shots are correctly and skillfully arranged, something extra is created that was not there before. This is what elevates recording events on film to an art form, and it is what we are always seeking. This is where the magic happens.

Tom Rolf, ACE, once explained that every film is really four films. There is the film as it is originally imagined by someone. Then there is the film written in script form, which leads to the third film, the one directed. The only film most people see is the film edited. There is a huge difference between the film imagined and the film edited.

The reason for this is that at every step in the process, creative people add something of themselves into the film. The person who imagined the film might also be the person who writes the script. But even if he or she is, the act of committing the idea to paper causes subtle changes in the material. Scripts usually go through many drafts before they are ready for the camera. Keep in mind also that the script is only a blueprint of the movie to come. It consists of stage directions and dialogue, with no real life of its own.

In a novel, the writer creates a whole world in the reader's imagination. In a script, it's bare bones. It is an opportunity waiting for craftsmen and actors to give life to it. Actor Louis Gossett, Jr., said, "If it were all in the script, there would be no point in making the movie." He is right, of course. It is the actor, the director, the cameraman, and all the other craftsmen who interpret the printed page.

After the script is committed to film, it comes to the cutting room, where the final interpretation takes place. When the film comes to me, I do not care what was written in the script. I only care about what went down on film. I still use the lined script for technical reasons, but my concern is to take the images given to me and raise them to a higher level. I must breathe life into the images and make my audience truly believe that what they are seeing is real, even though they know that it is not.

Years ago at RKO Studios there was a supervising film editor named Billy Hamilton. He mentored the careers of such editors as Robert Wise, Mark Robson, John Sturges, and Robert Parrish. All of these editors went on to be directors, but they got their grounding in film from Billy. One of them asked him after completing a film what the next project would be. He indicated that it was called *Bringing Up Baby*. The young editor inquired what it was about, and Billy said that he didn't know.

"Didn't they give you a script?"

"Yes, but I haven't read it. I never read scripts."

"Why not?" the Editor asked, astonished.

"Well," Billy went on, "I once tried to run a script through a projector, and it didn't work."

Now that might seem absurd, but it illustrates a point. The script has value while shooting in guiding the filmmakers. Once the scene is committed to film, that value ends. Then it is the film itself that determines what the movie will be. It is the editor's job to let the film guide him to its proper conclusion.

Sometimes it's better to not cut at all, though nowadays it often seems that cutting is done merely for the sake of cutting. Michael Bay (*Pearl Harbor*, *Armageddon*) in many of his films seems to cut merely to create a rhythm, often at the sacrificing of the story. I regard Mr. Bay as the Antichrist of film editing.

Early in *Pearl Harbor* there is a scene where a father is trying to explain why he's such a son-of-a-bitch to his son. It should be a dramatic, emotional scene, but the many cuts in the sequence destroy the actor's performance while establishing an energetic rhythm. Ben Affleck was paid a goodly amount of money for his performance in that film. Unfortunately, I never saw it because of the constant cutting.

Some scenes should be fast-paced, but not the entire movie. An action scene lends itself to many cuts to enhance the action. A love scene, on the other hand, benefits more from slow cuts, focusing on the actors' performance and allowing emotions to develop.

Armageddon and *Deep Impact* are both films with a similar theme. They both are almost remakes of *When Worlds Collide*. Both are about large meteors striking the Earth. The first film, by Michael Bay, features an ensemble cast of really fine actors, led by

Bruce Willis. It has incredible special effects, yet I cannot remember a single moment from that film because of the frantic cutting. But I will remember to my dying day the scene in *Deep Impact* where Tea Leoni and Maximillian Schell, playing father and daughter, are standing on the beach, waiting to be engulfed by the onrushing tidal wave. Under Mimi Leder's direction, that film was edited in a normal fashion, allowing me to care for the characters.

This leads us to a discussion of Walter Murch, ACE's, Rule of Six, which is best explained in his book *In the Blink of an Eye*. Without going into great detail, he contends that the most important reason to make a cut is for emotion. I agree completely. Emotion is what makes us watch the film and keeps us watching. The second reason is for story. We cut to advance the story. Rhythm is third on the list. The other three reasons are more technical in nature, and they are best explained by Murch in his brilliant book.

So, now we are faced with taking the film given us by the director and putting it together in a way that is emotional, tells a story, has a rhythm, and elevates the material to a higher plane, where we create something greater than the sum of the parts that were shot. Should be easy.

Chapter 4

Setting Up the Project

T o begin editing digitally, we need to set up the project. In the Avid, it is relatively simple. After starting the software, when the "select project" window comes up, you do exactly that. You click "new project," and a box opens, in which you can select what type of project you are doing. What is the format? If you select 24p, it will ask you if this is a film project. If it is, you select 16 mm or 35 mm; 35 can be either 4 perf or 3 perf.

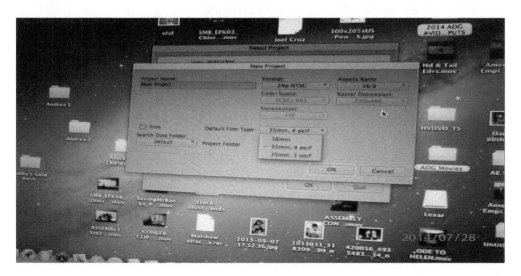

Figure 4.1. Setting up a project in Avid

If the project is digital, there is a multitude of formats to choose from. When you have accomplished this, name the project and open it. The Avid consists of three primary windows. The "project" window is where all of your bins reside. The "composer" window consists of two windows: a "source" window, in which you can view clips, and a "record" window, in which the cut footage plays. The third window is the "timeline," which shows all the events that are being cut together in a graphic that much resembles film running through a synchronizer. In the project window, there will be one bin with the name of the project on it. That will be your first capture bin.

If you are coming from tape, either transferred film or something originating on tape, you name the bin with the name of the tape. For example, if this were film dailies, the first tape would probably be called VT001 (videotape 1), and its time code would begin with hour one. If there were a second tape, it would be VT002, and the time code would start at hour two, and so on. VT002 would go in a separate bin.

Normally, you would receive a flex file from the transfer facility, either on DVD or by email. The flex file is the database for your footage. It is the same as the code book on a show that is cut on film. It contains all the information in regard to each shot. That would include the film key numbers, the time code of the tape, and the sound time code, as well as the scene and take number and date.

The flex file ends with the designation .flx. Normally, on an Avid show, there will also be an .ale file. If not, the .flx file can be translated into an .ale file through the Avid Log Exchange program in the Avid. After all, .ale stands for "Avid log exchange." The .ale file can be imported into the project and placed in the appropriate bin. VT001.ale would obviously go into bin VT001.

Installed in the bin would be all the data relating to the media on tape VT001. It would list every shot with the accompanying data. By highlighting the clips and selecting "batch capture," the Avid will automatically go through the tape and grab each clip by its time code. All clips will begin on an "A" frame, which will be discussed later.

If your project is tape-based, you will have to enter much of the data manually. You can go through the tape in "log in" mode and record the start and end of each clip, creating a database. Then you can batch capture. You can also capture the whole tape as a single clip and then go through and subclip it into individual shots.

Once the day's footage is captured into the correct bins, the work really begins. These are assistant editor duties, and they are extremely important. Let's assume that this is a film project, so all of the data must be accurate in relating back to the film negative.

The first task of the assistant film editor is to verify the database. The rule of "garbage in, garbage out" should be kept in mind. The assistant clicks the first clip up into the source window. There will be two or three window burns in the frame. One will contain the time code of the tape, the second will contain key numbers, and the third, if there is sound, will be the original sound time code.

At the top of the composer window on the right side of the source window above the frame is a place where your various tracks are indicated. Normally you would have V1, A1, and A2, which are video 1, audio 1, and audio 2. There is room only for two tracks. V1 should be clicked. By holding down the mouse, you can select source and key numbers. In this manner you can see your key numbers above the window and in the window burn. They should be exactly the same number.

Figure 4.2. Source window showing matching key numbers.

The number above the window is the database and indicates what the Avid believes to be the frame. The window burn is created by a bar code reader as the film is being telecined. If there is a discrepancy, it is more likely with the database than with the window burn. However, I would not assume anything. If there is a discrepancy, I would call the negative cutter and ask him or her to run down to a distinct frame on the negative of the shot (where the slate closes would be good) and tell me what the key number reads.

Whatever the case, I would have the telecine house redo the shot so that data and window burn match. Again, it can't be garbage in, garbage out. If errors are not caught at this stage, the consequences could be catastrophic. Negative will be cut from a list, and the list has to be completely accurate.

The numbers should be checked at the beginning of the shot, in the middle, and at the end. This must be done to all clips on a daily basis. This is the single most important thing the assistant does. After all the clips have been verified, they need to be copied to a temp bin for dispersal.

To do this, you can select all (Apple A) and hold down the option key and drag to the temp bin. Then the daily bin is closed, leaving a record of what came from the tape and a backup if a clip is lost. The temp bin is essentially a dispersal bin. From here clips are sorted into individual scene bins. When everything is moved from the temp bin to the scene bins, the temp is empty, waiting for the next day's tapes.

Why use a temp bin, you might ask? Why not just copy the shots directly from the daily bin into the scene bins? The reason is this: assistants are asked to do many things during the day, and it is rare that they are left to complete a task uninterrupted. By using the temp bin, you can always tell where you are. When the bin is empty, you know that you have dispersed all of the day's scenes.

In the scene bin the various clips are arranged in order by clicking on name in text mode by hitting Apple E. Once they are sorted in text mode, you can switch to frame mode. The images are small, but should be enlarged by hitting Apple L. They can then be resorted by clicking on the hamburger at the bottom of the scene bin and selecting "fill sorted." At this point the image of each clip can be manipulated by highlighting the clip and hitting the number 2 key at the top of the keyboard, which will move the clip forward eight frames at a time. You need to pick a frame that most indicates what the clip is about. This is so that when the editor opens the bin, he can immediately see what coverage he has for the scene.

When this has been done to all of the clips that have come in, the project is ready for editing. True, more material may come in the future for any of these scenes, but it can be integrated in the same way that the original clips were. As a rule, I try to edit whatever comes in on any given day. I do not wait for a scene to be complete. I cut what I have, and as new material appears, I incorporate it.

I use this system of bins regardless of what digital system I am working on. It's good for Final Cut Pro and Premiere as well as Avid. The important thing is to have a system where you can check your work and stay organized.

If you are working from a tape that does not come from film, it's even easier. The main thing is to be able to back track to the original tape. Now things are becoming file-based, and all you have is that file. You do need to know what to do if for some reason that file becomes corrupted or lost. This means backing it up in another place some way. You need to know how to recapture it and where it goes.

Once you have your daily and scene bins set up, you need to add some bins. I usually create folders in the project window for dailies and scenes. I then put the appropriate bins under the correct folders. You need a "cut footage" bin to keep your cuts. Also, there should be a "titles and opticals" bin, a "music" bin, and a "sound effects" bin. Again, this all goes back to organization. With all this in place, the project is set up, and the editor is ready to begin his work.

Before we continue on, we need to take a look at how all of this began and how that relates to what we do today.

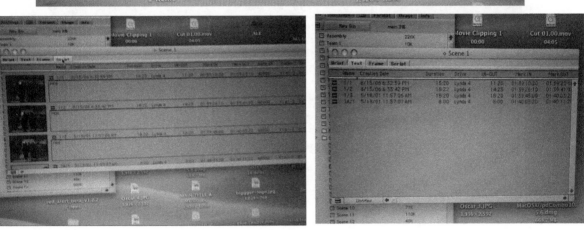

Figure 4.3. Three Shots: 1. In frame mode, the editor can see his coverage. 2. In script mode, the editor can make notes. 3. In text mode, the editor can see the data.

Chapter 5   *Early History*

A s the nineteenth century began to draw to its conclusion, the world was changing. Thomas Alva Edison had brought electric light to the city of New York. A subway to relieve congestion was being proposed, and the horseless carriages could be seen on the streets. Technology was having a large, ever-expanding effect on the lives of people everywhere.

The big hit of 1896 that had crowds lining up on those electric-lighted streets of New York was a moving picture called *The Kiss*. It ran all of forty-five seconds and featured two rather portly people doing lip locks on screen. The two lovers were John Rice and May Irwin, and the kiss was from the Broadway play they were acting in, *The Widow Jones*. The Edison Company filmed this short moment from the play, and the screen embrace was born. There was no sound. The entire film consisted of a single medium close-up, and there were no cuts.

Figure 5.1. The screen embrace is born in THE KISS (1896), Edison.

The Kiss is at the complete opposite end of the spectrum of editing from *The Horse Whisperer*. The former has no cuts at all, and the latter derives much of its power from the arrangement of the cuts. Between these two films lies nearly a century of editors developing and learning their craft. In 1896 filmmaking was all uncharted territory.

Motion pictures are possible because of a human phenomenon called "persistence of vision." This refers to the fact that the brain retains a visual image for an instant longer than the eye records it. This "flaw" allows the eye to view a series of progressive still images, which the brain blends together and interprets as moving pictures. In the nineteenth century, the discovery of this curiosity led to the development of such machines as the zoetrope, which was a revolving drum with a series of progressive pictures on it that gave the illusion of motion. It was essentially a toy, but it led to the development of the first motion picture cameras by the end of the century.

Figure 5.2. Zoetrope.

On the West Coast, in California, an English adventurer named Eadweard Muybridge had arrived there on the coat tails of the Gold Rush to make his fortune. He was an imaginative and innovative man who got into photography and in 1868 became famous for his large photographs of the Yosemite Valley. These pictures were composites made by using several smaller ones. He signed them "Helios—the Flying Studio."

At about the same time, Leland Stanford, the former governor of California (1861–1863), had invested in the Transcontinental Railroad and made his fortune. He became president of the Central Pacific Railroad. He also had a passion for horses. He bred them and raced them. He made a wager with a friend that at some point as a horse trotted, all four feet were off the ground. Stanford was determined to prove this.

In 1872, he hired Muybridge to help him win this wager with the use of a camera. His early attempts failed because his camera's shutter was not fast enough to freeze the horse's legs. Muybridge had to put the project aside temporarily because he was charged with the murder of his wife's lover. Though the charge was never proven and he was found not guilty, Muybridge decided that it was best that he spend some time in Mexico and Central America. There he made a living photographing publicity shots for the Union Pacific Railroad, which was owned by his employer, Leland Stanford.

In 1877, Muybridge succeeded in helping Stanford win the bet. He had developed a special shutter that exposed at two one-thousandths of a second. Muybridge set up a series of twelve to twenty-four still cameras and trip wires to trigger their shutters as a trotting horse passed to capture on film the proof of his employer's assertion. Stanford was right. At one point all four legs were off the ground. The series of still photographs proved the point, and Stanford collected $25,000. Aside from helping the governor win his bet, Muybridge discovered that he could reconstruct the motion of the horse by mounting his stills on a revolving wheel and projecting them through a magic lantern projector.

Muybridge continued shooting and projecting these moving pictures, but they were not real motion pictures because they came from separate cameras. Nevertheless, he developed his own lantern, the zoopraxiscope, which could project rapidly a series of photographs printed on a rotating glass disc. Muybridge toured the country and Europe lecturing on motion. It was featured at the 1893 World's Columbian Exposition in Chicago.

Figure 5.3. Birth of motion photography.

From 1884 to 1887, Muybridge made a study of motion for the University of Pennsylvania. He made a series of photographs of human figures in motion that became a source of study for scientists and artists. Some of them were published in a portfolio that was widely sold. A good deal of the attraction was photos of nude women performing various motions. In 1900, having opened the door into another world, he retired back to England, where he died in 1904.

In France, Etienne-Jules Marey, a physician, opened the door a step further. Besides inventing the sphygmograph, an instrument for recording pulse and blood pressure, he wrote extensively on such subjects as blood circulation and locomotion. In 1882, he built a photographic rifle to study the flight of birds. It recorded twelve images in one second on a single glass plate. This was the first series of photographs made by a single camera. It was an improvement, but very limited in terms of what it could capture.

In 1888, an Englishman working for Edison, William Kennedy Laurie Dickson, invented the Kinetograph, which became known as the Edison motion-picture camera. The Edison Vitascope, or projector, was subsequently invented by Thomas Armat. Edison himself was not particularly interested in any of these things, though he did take the time to patent them in his name. He was more interested in his phonograph, but his employee Dickson saw the power inherent in motion pictures.

None of this would have gone much further without the help of an American named George Eastman. After working for an insurance company, in 1880 he developed a process of making dry plates for photography. He also developed a transparent film and in 1884, founded the Eastman Dry Plate and Film Company. In 1888, he invented the Kodak still camera, which brought photography to the public. It was purchased with a one-hundred-exposure roll of film inside, and after shooting the camera was sent to Eastman for processing and reloading. In 1892 the company was reorganized as the Eastman Kodak Company. In 1900, the Brownie camera was introduced for children.

Eastman had recently invented celluloid roll film. Dickson, with his Kinetograph, decided to record his images on this new product instead of on wax cylinders, as had been done in the past. The film ran through the camera at 48 frames per second, and Dickson came up with the idea of adding four perforations on either side of each frame to guide the film through the machine.

In 1889, William Dickson used his newly invented camera to photograph on George Eastman's film stock an Edison employee sneezing. *Fred Ott's Sneeze* became the first film made in the United States. Dickson's camera was imitated and improved upon by innovators around the world. Soon, enthusiasts everywhere were photographing and projecting moving pictures and making their own contributions to progress.

The motion picture film industry actually began on December 28, 1895, in the basement of the Paris Grande café, when the Lumière brothers first exhibited one of their films to a paying public. Auguste and Louis Lumière were inventors who manufactured still cameras. They developed their own motion picture equipment and began shooting short scenes of daily life. Prior to this, the phenomenon of "moving pictures" had been a toy in the hands of its inventors. From the moment of this paid exhibition, the toy passed from the hands of interested innovators and artists to entrepreneurs, thieves, and scalawags.

The earliest filmmakers were the prisoners of time and space. Initially it was enough just to photograph moving objects and project them. A train arriving at the station, workers leaving an industrial plant, automobiles on the street, a fire engine—these were enough to thrill audiences eager to see the new "moving pictures." As the nineteenth century drew to a close, people were willing to pay to see the magic of the pictures that moved like real life. *The Kiss*, as discussed, was a scene from a play, and it was the forerunner of the narrative cinema that was to come.

France and England took the lead in the developing the medium artistically and commercially. The first film credited with having more than one scene was Robert W. Paul's *Come Along, Do!* It was made early in 1898 and consisted of two scenes joined together by a splice. The first scene showed a couple in a room of an art gallery, and it was followed by a second scene, in which they entered another room inside the gallery. Here was a beginning of continuity and story.

Today this does not seem like an innovative thing, but remember that prior to this, audiences were looking only at single moving shots. The idea of cutting from one shot to another was totally revolutionary in that it represented nothing that the eye normally sees. With our vision we see a continuous picture. There are no cuts. Cutting to something else was a very bold step. This innovation was the first step in elevating motion pictures to an art form.

George Albert Smith was a photographer in Brighton, England, who, like the Lumière brothers, built his own motion picture camera in 1896 and began making and selling films. At that time a phenomenon called "phantom rides" was popular. This was done by mounting a camera on front of a locomotive and filming the scenery from that point of view. It would then be projected for audiences. Many people did not travel or ride trains, and the view from the front of a train was worth paying money to see.

To enhance this experience, Smith came up with the idea of adding a shot of a couple kissing to be cut in when the train entered a tunnel. With the help of his wife, he filmed a short shot of a man kissing a woman in a railway car. People watching the "phantom ride" would then have the added titillation of seeing a kiss stolen in a train tunnel. The film of the kiss could also be purchased separately.

The success of this idea led James Bamforth to copy it with *The Kiss in the Tunnel*, which featured three shots. The first showed an actual train entering a tunnel. In the second shot a man is shown kissing a woman in a train compartment. This was a set. The final shot was the camera mounted on the front of the train, as on the "phantom ride," emerging from a tunnel. This was the beginning of "synthesis of time and space": three shots photographed at three separate times, in three locations, joined together to tell a very simple story.

So, by 1899 in Europe and Britain, fictional films were being created with more than one shot, though in the United States single-shot films were still being made. Beginning with the Lumière brothers, who photographed scenes of actual life in outdoor settings, European cinema, with notable exceptions, tended to be more reality-based and filmed on location. The Americans followed the lead of the Edison Company, which photographed on stages such as the famous "Black Maria" in New Jersey, which was a revolving building constructed to follow the sun. Rather than shoot life as it was, ingenious Americans preferred to build sets and stage action.

In 1902, in a notable exception to European style, the French magician Georges Méliès, who had been making films since 1896, produced his famous *Le Voyage Dans La*

Lune (A Trip to the Moon). This pioneer of special effects originally came from the stage and thought of films in theatrical terms. His movie is essentially a photographed stage play with special effects. The shots are all wide, as though one were observing a stage play. Each scene is complete in itself, and what cuts and/or dissolves there are take the audience forward from scene to scene, without the benefit of any cutting within a scene.

Méliès' film is entertaining at fourteen minutes, but, more important than that, it captured the public's imagination. Now, besides seeing pictures that moved, the audience was introduced to moving pictures that told an actual story. It received worldwide distribution, but the camera is stationary, and there is no pacing to the scenes. There are no close-ups or moving shots. It is not filmmaking as we know it, because the basic tool of filmmaking, the shot, was not understood as the building block to creating a scene.

It remained for Edwin S. Porter, the director of production at the Edison Film Company, to carry things even further back in the United States. Real editing begins with Porter. He was a cameraman who was hired by Edison in 1896. Initially he was assigned to set up Edison's Vitascope for film projection. Later, he worked as cameraman and general handyman before rising to the head of production. He was inspired by the possibilities of storytelling that Méliès had explored in *A Trip to the Moon*. In true American fashion, he felt that he could do better.

By 1901, he was head of production at Edison. Edison was covering the Pan-American Exposition in Buffalo, New York, at this time. President McKinley was visiting the event, and the Edison cameramen captured him on film. It was the last footage to be recorded of him, because, while there, he was assassinated by an anarchist. Quick to capture the moment, the cameramen filmed the emotions of the crowds at the exposition as they learned what had happened.

With that footage, and the funeral, the Edison Company, under Porter, made several films of the historic event. Taking it a step further, Porter asked for permission to film the execution of Leon Czolgosz, the assassin of President McKinley, in the electric chair. Porter was refused, so, undaunted, he decided to stage his own version. He captured a wide shot of Auburn State Prison and dissolved from that into the prison itself and finally into a staged execution of the prisoner. It was called *Execution of Czolgosz with Panorama of Auburn Prison*. The success of this venture probably inspired Porter to conceive a more important project.

Porter brought purpose to the new craft of editing. With *The Life of an American Fireman* (1903), Porter once again combined staged action with actual footage of a fire to tell the story of a mother and child trapped by a fire and saved by the firemen. He began by assembling actual footage of fire departments. Then he added new staged footage that he shot of the mother and child pretending to be trapped in a fire.

This was a big step in the birth of editing. In laying out his cuts, he had to assume that his audience could make the connections between a shot and the next shot following. Cutting from the stock footage of the firemen to the staged footage of the woman and child presupposed that the audience would understand that the firemen were trying to save the woman and child. At that time Porter was making a rather large supposition of what audiences would think.

But Porter was right. Audiences could follow his story. In combining the stock shots and the staged shots, he created a level of drama previously unknown. To the then-unsophisticated viewers, tension was created as to whether the woman and child would be rescued in time. When they were, the crowd felt immense relief. These feelings,

Figure 5.4. (A) Woman trapped by fire (staged).

Figure 5.4. (B) Firemen on way (real) in THE LIFE OF AN AMERICAN FIREMAN (1903), Edison.

which were manipulated solely by the arrangements of the cuts, were the forerunner of what we experienced in watching the accident scene edited by Hank Corwin, ACE, in *The Horse Whisperer*.

Porter had begun to understand that the shot was the basic building block of visual storytelling, just like the word is the basic building block of writing. By arranging his shots, both real and staged, in a certain order, he was able to create a more dramatic story. This use of "stock shots" and staged footage demonstrated the synthesis of time and space, as well as, in its effect on an audience, a whole that was greater than the sum of the parts.

Porter still did not understand pacing, however. Lengths of shots had nothing to do with their dramatic impact. Also, he didn't seem to have a problem with repeating action in two shots that cut together. If someone entered a building in an exterior and entered a second time in the interior cut, Porter saw no problem with it. It remained for others to solve the problem of this continuity error. Nevertheless, *The Life of an American Fireman* shows the beginnings of the power of editing.

It is important to note that none of these pioneers of editing existed in a vacuum. Experimentation was going on around the world. Filmmakers imitated each other shamelessly, and it is very difficult to say with any great authority who actually did what first. Porter's *American Fireman* draws very heavily from a film made in England in 1901 by James Williamson called *Fire!* This film is notable for its linking of action and different locations in a continuity of separate cuts. Porter's version is significant in his use of existing stock shots combined with staged action.

Later in 1903, Porter made *The Great Train Robbery*. At twelve minutes, it was twice the length of *Fireman*, and involved exteriors and interiors and the passage of time. Without the use of fades and dissolves, he was able to move the story from place to place and through time by not using whole shots. He also created "parallel action" in cutting from the robbers to the tied-up telegraph operator and eventually to the people who become the posse. By coming into an action in progress and leaving before completion, he was able to suggest changes in time and space. Porter's film told a story with its shots that represented a narrative continuity, and Porter himself became the first god of time and space.

In that same year of 1903, back in Brighton, England, G. A. Smith in *Mary Jane's Mishap* cut from a long shot to a medium shot and back to the long shot. It was a shot of a woman lighting a stove, and Smith made this cut in three times. Again, audiences were able to follow this departure from reality for the sake of story. Filmmakers were beginning to discover the three basic shots of filmmaking: the long shot, the medium shot, and the close-up.

Besides Smith, a whole group of innovative young filmmakers had sprung up in the Brighton area. Sometimes known as the School of Brighton, they included Smith, Cecil Hepworth, James Williamson, Charles Urban, and Esme Collings, among others. They experimented with close-ups, moving cameras, and editorial rhythms. One of the earliest known editors was Mabel Clark, who in 1905 edited *Rescued by Rover*, which was directed by Cecil Hepworth. It was one of the best edited films of the period, and Hepworth credits Clark in this area. The story is basically of a dog, Rover, rescuing a baby kidnapped by gypsies. Mabel actually played the nursemaid who loses the infant in the beginning of the film. Her editing added a great deal to the suspense of the production.

Now, the groundwork had been done, and the foundations were laid for the emergence of a giant who could integrate all of this together into a practical theory and set of rules for filmmaking and editing. He was to come from an unlikely source. Born in Kentucky in 1875, he considered himself to be a playwright and a stage actor. Acting in motion pictures was beneath him. But when he needed money, he was not above appearing in them. He was David Wark Griffith, and he was the father of film editing.

I have heard that his first appearance on camera was in *The Great Train Robbery*, as a member of the posse. The storyteller in me would like to believe this, but I can find no documentation to support the claim. It may not be true, but it doesn't really matter, because in 1907 he appeared as a lumberjack in Edwin S. Porter's film *Rescued from an Eagle's Nest*. Whichever film of Porter's he started with, he learned quickly that he could make a steady income in the film business, and by 1908 he began directing for Biograph.

Griffith was not eager to try his hand at directing. He had never even directed a stage play and was concerned about losing steady work as an actor if he failed in that capacity. He had been recommended by Arthur Marvin, one of two cameramen at Biograph (G. W. "Billy" Bitzer was the other), who was the brother of the general manager, Henry Marvin. His first film was *The Adventures of Dollie*, and the company was pleased with it, though in no way did it suggest the innovations that were to follow as the master learned his craft.

At this time most of the technical aspects of filmmaking were in the hands of either the cameraman or the director. Cameramen took their own film to the lab and after processing separated the good takes from the bad. Finished films were often assembled over a bench by the director or cameraman. There were no machines to view the film on, other than projectors, as they worked. The future gods of time and space were in those days called "patchers," and their main job was to hold the takes for the director or cameraman who was assembling the film, hand that person what was needed, and then "patch" the cut shots together with film cement.

As time went on, some of these patchers were allowed to take over the cutting of the films to leave the directors free to direct and the cameramen free to shoot. These cutters also acted as the script clerks on the set, keeping track of what was shot, which was invaluable to them when they reached the cutting room. Eventually patchers split into two roles: script supervisors and editors.

Patchers cut film with scissors, holding it up to examine against a light source and then marking and making the cut. Emulsion was scraped off with a razor blade, and cement was applied. The two pieces of film were held together until the splice dried.

Into this mysterious world came D. W. Griffith. Griffith's time at Biograph was a great learning experience. In 1908, in a seven-month period, he shot sixty-one films. Granted, they were only one-reelers (ten minutes in length), but they were stories. The next year he shot 141 films, and in his whole career he shot more than 500 films. By sheer volume alone, he was forced to learn and improve his craft.

Griffith may not have invented all of the techniques he is given credit for, but he intuitively understood what they meant, which was far more important. At the dawn of recorded history, man learned to arrange words into sentences, sentences into paragraphs, and paragraphs into stories. He learned how to communicate with the written word his ideas, emotions, and stories. He developed punctuation to make his meanings clear. It was Griffith who did this for film.

He began to grasp the correct manner of arranging shots to tell a story and that altering their lengths could build tension and heighten emotions. In his ninth film, made in mid-1908, he began perfecting what would become known as the "Griffith last-minute rescue." In *The Fatal Hour*, a woman is tied to a bed with a gun pointed at her, with the gun rigged to a clock that will fire the weapon at twelve o'clock. Griffith cut between the girl, the clock, and her would-be rescuers racing to save her. The cutting heightened the tension in much the same way as this technique did in *The Life of an American Fireman*, though at a greater level.

Griffith understood that the arrangements of shots could suggest relationships not inherent in the shots by themselves. In *A Corner in Wheat* (1909), he cut between poor people turned away from a bread line because they can't afford the price and a wheat baron giving a lavish dinner for his friends. This arrangement of cuts showed the contrast between the rich and poor and made a powerful statement about it. During his Biograph period, Griffith experimented with extreme long shots (*Ramona*), the close-up and cutaway *(Enoch Arden)*, dramatic time *(The Lonely Villa)*, tracking shots *(The Lonedale Operator)*, and variations of pace.

By the end of 1911, Griffith began making longer pictures. He felt that audiences could watch a story that extended beyond the standard one-reel format. He remade *Enoch Arden* as a two-reeler. He met a certain amount of resistance from the Biograph executives in his desire to lengthen his stories and initially had to release the picture in two parts. Audiences eventually demanded that the picture be shown as a single film.

Biograph had, at the end of 1908, joined the Motion Picture Patents Company, also known as the Trust. This group also included such companies as Edison, Vitagraph, Essanay, Selig, Pathé Frères, Kalem, Lubin, and Méliès. These companies controlled most of the motion picture patents of the time and came together to control the market. They felt that two reels should be the limit for a film. In 1915 they were eventually declared in federal court to be an illegal conspiracy in restraint of trade.

In the beginning of the twentieth century, filmmaking had become a business. The business entrepreneurs were in charge. Originally films had been sold to projectionists, who traveled around the country, exhibiting them in vaudeville houses. But theaters began popping up that ran films on a regular basis. By 1908, there were thousands of theaters, and the demand for new films was gigantic. Each theater usually ran a program of about an hour featuring six different one-reelers. It was no longer practical to buy films. Rental was the answer, and the Trust set up its own distribution arm called the General Film Company.

There was opposition to the Trust from the independents. They chose to make their films in whatever manner they chose and at whatever length. Among them were Carl Laemmle, who was to found Universal Pictures, and William S. Fox, who would found the Fox Company. The Trust would not allow George Eastman to sell his raw stock to anyone outside of the group, nor would it rent films to theaters who rented from independents.

To escape this monopoly, many of these producers came to Southern California, where the weather was sunny and the scenery varied. There was less control there, and it was easier to come by the Eastman raw stock. These producers filed suit against the Motion Picture Patents Company and the General Film Company and began setting up their own distribution and theater chains. It was their suits that eventually brought down the Trust.

In 1910, Griffith had convinced Biograph to let him shoot part of the time in California. Again in 1911 he was allowed to come west, and that is where *The Lonedale Operator* was shot. Griffith still wanted to make longer, "feature-length" films, but the Trust was against it. In France *Queen Elizabeth* (1912) was a full fifty-three minutes, and Italy's *Quo Vadis?* (1913) was feature-length, at eight reels.

Griffith was frustrated that Biograph and the Trust were limiting the length of his films. When he came to California in 1913, he decided to make a feature-length biblical epic without consulting the executives. In the San Fernando Valley he created a huge set for *Judith of Bethalia* and went about making his movie at the length he felt it justified. Management at Biograph was outraged, and Griffith was told that he could not continue directing films for the company. *Judith* was cut down to four reels, and Griffith chose to leave. He made a deal with Mutual Reliance-Majestic, which included permission to make two independent features per year in addition to those contracted.

Two producers who had been associated with Griffith at Biograph had left the studio a year earlier. They were Thomas Ince and Mack Sennett. Both of these protégés had an effect on the future of editing. Ince leased a parcel of land in the Santa Ynez Canyon, which became known as Inceville, and began grinding out Westerns with an emphasis on action. He wrote, directed, and edited his early films and even acted in them. He was very focused in his cutting and cut out anything that didn't move the action along.

In Ince's 1912 film *The Invaders*, directed by Francis Ford, the concept of the reverse shot was introduced. A couple sitting and talking in the outdoors are being stalked by a rejected lover. The scene is presented with the stalker in the foreground and the couple in the rear, and then a cut is made to the reverse, to show the couple in the foreground and the stalker in the background. This is repeated several times.

Mack Sennett opened the Keystone Company and began making comedies. Comedy more than any other genre helped put an end to the photographed stage-play look of movies. Comedies relied on nonstop action. To retain its audience, a comedy had to set up a joke quickly and deliver it fast. Sennett became a master of this, and at his factory the rhythm of editing was changing.

Into this madcap environment walked a young man named William Hornbeck. He came to Keystone first as "film wrapper," winding film in the studio's lab. He moved on to be a printer and eventually a projectionist. In that job, as he projected several versions, evolving from the raw footage to the final cut, he began to understand how editing worked. When World War I began, he was promoted to editor. He had learned his craft well, and by 1921 he was the head of the department.

Hornbeck was destined to go on to edit in England during the 1930s, run post at Universal, and work for George Stevens. For Stevens he edited the Americana trilogy of *A Place in the Sun*, *Shane*, and *Giant*.

In 1914 a theatrical producer and playwright name Cecil B. DeMille came out to California to make a film called *The Squaw Man*. With cofounder Jesse L. Lasky, he made this the first release of the Famous Players Company, which was to become Paramount Pictures. DeMille understood the importance of editing and actually edited his first films.

In 1915, Margaret Booth, who was to have one of the longest careers in film editing, went to work for Griffith as a patcher. She had to supplement her family's income when her brother, an actor named Elmer Booth, was killed in an auto accident. She learned to cut negative. In those days there were no key numbers on the negative to match up to. It all had to be done by eyeballing to match.

Margaret was to become the most powerful film editor who ever lived. She eventually went to work for Louis B. Mayer and followed him into the newly formed Metro-Goldwyn-Mayer (MGM).

There she met Irving Thalberg, who was the first person to use the title "film editor," and he applied it to her. Mayer and Thalberg trusted Booth's story instincts, and she became the final word on the studio's pictures. If she didn't like the way a film ended, she had the power to demand that a new ending be shot.

Margaret Booth died in 2002 at the age of 104. She had lived in three centuries and had seen it all. The last film she took an editing credit on was *Annie*, in 1989. I attended her funeral in Beverly Hills, along with the studio heads who had known her. I talked to one of the mourners, who said to me, "She invented pacing. She was the first."

Griffith, in 1915, made his epic film *The Birth of a Nation*. It combined all the lessons he had learned over the years about filmmaking, storytelling, and editing. It is the foundation of American film. Today it gets a bad rap because of its depiction of African Americans, but that is not the point. The point is that it's a great piece of filmmaking. So is *The Battleship Potemkin*, which is very obviously a communist film. We can appreciate it without supporting communism.

Figure 5.5. The foundation of American film, THE BIRTH OF A NATION (1915), Griffith.

Taken aback by some of the negative reactions to the film, Griffith was inspired to make an even bigger epic with *Intolerance*. Telling five different stories in five different time periods, all on the subject of intolerance, it was ahead of its time in structure. No one attempted that kind of storytelling again for more than eighty years, until the release of *The Hours* and *Cloud Atlas*.

As the 1920s began, film was becoming fairly sophisticated, but there was still no editing machine. It was still a matter of holding up film to the light, cutting it with

Figure 5.6. Ahead of its time: INTOLERANCE (1916), Griffith.

scissors, and gluing it together. An innovation was needed. It came from an unusual source.

Iwan Serrurier was an electrical engineer from Holland. Early in the twentieth century, he married his sweetheart, and they came to the United States on their honeymoon. They attended the 1904 World's Fair in St. Louis and were particularly taken with the California Exhibit. They decided to move there.

Iwan and his wife purchased land in what is now Altadena and began raising children. He worked for the power company and then later the railroad, but in his spare time he became fascinated with movie projectors. He imagined building a device on which people could watch movies in a cabinet in their own homes. He built a number of these machines and even sold a few.

One Friday, Iwan tried to interest an executive at the Doug Fairbanks Studio in his invention for watching dailies. The executive wasn't interested because he had a perfectly good screening room for this. So, Iwan, rather despondent, walked across the studio lot toward the gate. On the way he passed a cutting room where patchers were holding up film to the light, making cuts, and gluing pieces together.

He asked one of the patchers whether it would be easier if he had a viewing machine. The patcher said it would, and at that moment Iwan was touched by the hand of God. He had an inspiration that would change the craft of editing forever. He went home and retooled his machine into a wooden box with a crank and a large magnifier for viewing the film to be cranked through it. He took it back to Fairbanks and sold it to Fairbanks himself for $125. It was the first Moviola.

Soon other studios wanted the invention, and Iwan Serrurier was in the Moviola business. The name came from a contest he had with his kids to name it. "Moviola" was based on "Victrola," the name of the original phonograph player. There was some

Figure 5.7. The original Moviola.

resistance among editors to using the machine, because you were cranking cellulose nitrate (film) over a heat source, and it was highly flammable. Just the same, the advantages of the machine were numerous. Patchers became editors because they were able to audition cuts on the machine and change them before committing to negative cutting.

By this time it became standard practice to make a work print of the original negative for editing purposes. With the work print and the Moviola, it was easy to put the picture together, try various ways of cutting, and arrive at the best possible version. Then the work print could be given to a negative cutter, who would conform the negative to match the cuts in the work print. This was made easier by the use of key numbers.

Eastman began recording numbers on the raw stock as a latent image. These numbers became visible when the negative was developed. When the work print was made, the numbers would print through and then could be used in matching negative to print.

Iwan Serrurier was a dedicated craftsman. Every Moviola was handmade. The machine was ordered, and the editor had to wait while it was built to his specifications.

Figure 5.8. Original key numbers.

In 1973 I bought my first Moviola through Christy's Editorial in Burbank. I described how I wanted it, and then I had to wait while it was built. It cost $3,000. That's how every Moviola was made until they stopped being manufactured in the 1990s.

Credits

Fig. 5.2: Copyright © Andrew Dunn (CC BY-SA 2.0) at http://en.wikipedia.org/wiki/File:Zoetrope.jpg.
Fig. 5.3: Eadweard Muybridge, 1878.
Fig. 5.7: Source: http://www.city-net.com/~fodder/edit/moviola.html.
Fig. 5.8: Copyright © LACameraman (CC BY-SA 3.0) at http://en.wikipedia.org/wiki/File:Keykode-edgecode.jpg.

Chapter 6 Getting Started

Y ou sit at the Avid facing a blank screen. The first day's dailies are loaded, and you are ready to begin. What will the all-important first shot be? How will you start the film? Chances are that what you start editing won't be the opening of the movie. You begin with the first scene that has been shot. It was chosen because of factors of economics and availability of actors and sets. The cast is not performing the film in continuity, so why should you be working in continuity? You take what's available.

The first thing you should do is view all the dailies in the scene bin before you and not on the Avid. I like to work to a fifty-two-inch screen or larger. I have my Avid hooked up to one. It's not the optimum way to view your dailies. It should be on the big screen, like God and DeMille intended. But nowadays that's not an option that we have very often. So, you make do by watching on the largest screen available.

The old days, when we saw our dailies in a screening room, were the best. You watched the performances play out as they would in a theater, and you could make accurate judgments. I usually walked out of dailies having cut the picture in my mind. It would then take several hours to create, either on film or in the Avid, what was in my head.

Normally I would have notes from the director of his impressions as we watched the dailies. I read these, but basically I follow my instincts. If we disagree about which is the best take, I may go with my choice if I feel strongly about it, but I need to be able to defend that choice. When I was editing *Hail Caesar* for director Anthony Michael Hall, I picked a certain take, which I felt was overall the best take in terms of camera and performance. Michael preferred another take because he felt that his performance in the other take was better. It was his film, so we went with his choice. In retrospect I feel that he was right: performance is more important than camera work.

Figure 6.1. Author editing with Anthony Michael Hall.

Having now viewed all the material for your scene, you are ready to begin. You have created a cut footage bin, and it is open. When you put up the first clip in the source bin, mark an in and out, and go to "splice in"; the program will ask you which bin to put it in. Once you have selected "cut footage," the sequence will reside in that bin.

After marking an in and out on the clip, I often preview the cut by striking the 6 key at the top of the keyboard or by striking the key under the play key on the source monitor. This will play the clip from in mark to out mark. I do this to see how it feels on my big monitor. I may adjust either the in or the out mark and play it again. Satisfied, I will hit the yellow "splice in" button and commit to the cut.

After making the first cut, I must decide what the next thing is that I want to show my audience. What is the next information I want to give to them? Each scene has a purpose in the movie. There is a reason for it being in the script. I know what the purpose is, and my job is to achieve this purpose through my manner of arranging the cuts. I industriously go about doing this.

I try to match action as I cut from one shot to the next. Sometimes this can be easily accomplished, and sometimes not. Part of the script supervisor's job is to keep track of the continuity and make sure that the actor always picks up the object with the same hand. Sometimes this doesn't work out. If you cut correctly on action, you can often fake out the audience. I have often cut from a wide shot of an actor reaching with his left hand and picking it up in a close-up with the right hand. If the action moves smoothly, at the same speed, no one will notice.

You do have to be careful in cutting on action. You need a little overlap of action, or the eye won't see it correctly. If you cut it too tight, it is too fast to register. If it looks good when you play it, it is good even if there are overlapping frames in there.

Besides matching action in your construction, you need to keep in mind Walter Murch's first three rules for cutting: emotion, story, and rhythm. You are telling a story, and you are leading your audience through it. At all times you need to make the story interesting and engaging as you impart information to the viewer. And you need it to have a rhythm.

L.A. Confidential is a complex story that takes well over two hours to tell. It is so well edited by Peter Honess, ACE, that the movie seems to fly by and is over very quickly. Thelma Schoonmaker, ACE, with *The Departed* created a very exciting pace that drives a story that is two and a half hours long. Both films are examples of the triumph of editing expertly using emotion, story, and rhythm to create a whole greater than the sum of the parts.

Eventually you shape your material together into what you feel is the best possible scene. This may require trying things and rejecting them when they don't work. I push ahead with emotion and story. Rhythm usually comes from the material itself. When you are finished, you put away the scene in the cut footage bin. Label it with the scene number and move on to the next available scene.

Once you have made your cut, leave it alone. There will be time to rework it when you join it up to other scenes. In this first cut you will make two passes with the footage. First, you cut the individual scenes. Then, as you have scenes that belong together, you begin connecting them and seeing how they work in continuity. This may affect scenes when you see them together. Sometimes things that are not necessary can be removed to make the film flow better.

In the first or editor's cut, you are obligated to show the director every scene he shot in the order intended, but when running in continuity individual shots may be changed or eliminated. Because we are working digitally, an alternate version can be created at the same time that may play better. Bonnie Koehler, ACE, did this, and after running the cut for the director, she would ask whether he would like to see the film as she thought it should be, and if he said, "Yes," she would show him the alternate version.

As you move through the film, you develop a relationship with it. You become as one. This is very much like a love affair. You meet someone and become attracted. You begin dating and become lovers. As the editing continues, you are in tune with the footage. You take the best from it and give it your best.

When I worked on film, I often would project my cuts to watch them on the big screen. In doing so I could hone and polish the footage to a great extent before running my cut for the director. Often, when I had a few reels together, I would watch them with my assistants and get a feel for audience reaction.

Now I am somewhat limited in how I watch my cuts but I can output to DVD and go to a screening room. My former assistant, Nancy Brindley Bhagia, when she was cutting *Alien Hunger*, would make Blu-rays and view her work through her husband's video projection system on a ten-foot screen. It goes back to what Robert Wise told me about Orson Welles watching scenes of *Citizen Kane* on the big screen. He was the audience; Nancy was the audience, and you should be the audience, too.

On a big screen, it plays differently. We learned this working on the Moviola. If it was slow on the Moviola, it would be death on the big screen. That's why cuts were watched in a theater, to get the proper experience. When I cut my first Avid film, *To the Ends of Time*, I made the producer run it on the big-screen TV that he had in his apartment.

As you move forward with the cut, you encounter many different types of scenes. Many of them are dialogue scenes, because most often it is dialogue that drives the story forward. The thing to keep in mind is what the point is at any given moment that you are trying to make. That determines whether you are showing the speaker, the listener, or somewhere else when a line is spoken.

Experienced editors agree that the hardest scene to cut is the dining room scene. Everyone is seated and the action is minimal, so the challenge is to keep it interesting and exciting despite the lack of action. A good example is the HBO film *Conspiracy*, which is a dramatic re-creation of the Wannsee Conference that occurred in 1942. For an hour and a half several Nazis sat around a dining room table deciding the "final solution" of the Jewish question. There is no real action. It is all dialogue, and Peter Zinner, ACE, kept it moving and compelling.

Action scenes provide a great break from dialogue because they are pure visualization. You need to create an exciting rhythm while letting your audience know what is happening, without holding any cut for very long. Some editors are very good at this and specialize in it, but as editors we have to deal with the picture as a whole and make it play throughout.

I have been speaking of rhythm to a great degree. In many current films music plays an important part in telling the story. There is a tendency among inexperienced editors to cut to music. *Never do this unless you are cutting a musical number.* Narrative editors never cut to music. You cut for the natural rhythms of the scene inherent in the actors' performance, the camera work, and the directing. Cutting to music will throw this off. Keep in mind that the composer works for the picture, not the other way around.

Donn Cambern, ACE, when he was cutting *Easy Rider*, had many memorable scenes in which popular songs enhanced the story. None of these scenes, many of which were traveling scenes, were cut to music. They were cut solely for the film's natural rhythm, and then various songs were tried with them. When one seemed to fit, it was used, and possibly some cuts were adjusted to hit on a beat. Picture cutting leads, and sound follows to enhance. That is the pecking order.

Sometimes natural rhythms are altered for specific reasons. In Howard Hawks's *Red River*, edited by Christian Nyby, the start of the cattle drive is shaped into an artificial rhythm to create excitement. It starts with very slow shots, until John Wayne tells Montgomery Cliff to give the signal to start. This leads to a series of quick cuts of cowboys yelling and beginning the drive.

The effect of this on the big screen is dynamic. Somehow it draws the audience into the cattle drive. When Nyby's son was taking film classes at USC, he read about the power of this sequence in Karel Reiz's book *The Technique of Film Editing*. He asked his father whether he understood all of the emotions he was creating in the sequence. Nyby replied, "Hell no. It just looked good."

That says a lot. Often we make a cut and it just looks good. It feels right. So we go with it. Montages are created with a special rhythm to serve a special purpose of one kind or another. Often tension is created in the lengths of cuts leading up to a dramatic moment or action. It's all storytelling to create an emotional response in the audience.

Chapter 7

The First Cut

E ventually the shooting will finish, and the pressure will be on you to deliver the first cut of the picture. This is potentially a very stressful time for the editor. When I was cutting *Illusions* for Victor Kulle, he asked me to show him the picture before running for the producer and the executives. I booked two screenings, one right after the other. Victor arrived, and we both entered the screening room. We sat a few seats apart. The picture began, and I watched him for any signs. I saw none. The picture ended, and the lights came up. Victor walked out without saying a word.

I thought, "*This is it. I'm going to be fired. He doesn't like it.*" I started thinking about what I would do while I was out of work. Then the producer, Steven Paul, arrived. He and his entourage walked in. Victor and I followed. The lights went down, and the picture began again. Steven's reactions were fairly immediate. He loved it. He made comments from time to time, but he seemed to feel that we had a picture.

It wasn't until much later that I realized that Victor must have had the same uncertainty about his work as I had about mine. He and I were both waiting to be validated, and Steven Paul did that for both of us. I had probably been cutting for ten years before I felt that I knew what I was doing. Michael Kahn, ACE, Steven Spielberg's editor, told me that he had felt the same way. Early on I would run my cuts secretly for my friend Cecelia Hall before I showed them to the director. She would validate me and point out problems that I needed to address.

Even now when I run a first cut, I get butterflies. So much can go wrong. And sometimes what seemed good on paper just doesn't work on the big screen. I learned early on to rehearse before a screening. My first assistant, John Hanson, taught me that. He had assisted on both David Lean's *Ryan's Daughter* and Francis Ford Coppola's *Godfather II*. When I was cutting *Flatbed Annie and Sweetiepie: Lady Truckers*, a Movie of the Week for CBS, we screened the picture in its entirety before running it for the producer and director. We made sure that the projectionist was showing the film properly and changing reels unseen.

It has been my policy to rehearse at least part of the picture before I have a screening for anyone of note. We are in show business, and first impressions count. If a screening starts off badly, the picture will look bad, no matter how well you've cut it. The first cut is where everyone has their chance to panic, and editors are usually the first to get fired.

So, when you are going to run your first cut, be ready. If you are not, ask for more time. Do whatever it takes to get extra time, because your job depends on it. Even when we were still working on film, I would lay some sound effects and music to enhance the viewing. If we couldn't afford a temp mix, I would go to a room where you could run extra tracks and do a live mix.

On the Avid it's easy. I often let my assistant lay sound effects for me, and I cut in temp music that fits the mood of the scene. I certainly don't let an MOS (silent) sequence play without something covering it. It's easy to do a mix and then output it for viewing. Never, ever let a scene play with holes in the track, director cues, or anything that will take the viewer out of the moment. Again, we are in show business, and it's our job to give them a show.

You need to pace yourself so that you have time to make the picture look good for the first screening. That's why I cut everything I can when it comes in. Always try to make your cuts just like you want them to play in a theater. There are no rough cuts. We make every cut as close as possible to what we think it should be. Sure, some sequences will get shorter eventually, but always cut as though this will be the final cut.

The first reel, the middle, and the end are the most important. I'm not suggesting that you ignore other reels, but in the first ten minutes the viewer either accepts or rejects the film. Buyers who are picking films for their territories often look only at the first reel and move on. I have often found that in the first thirty minutes of a film, there is an extra ten minutes that should come out. This won't happen on the first cut, but you still need the opening to stand tall and strut.

Somewhere in the middle there needs to be a really memorable scene, and the ending should have the audience on the edge of their seats. Sam Peckinpah's *The Wild Bunch* is a good example of a film that covers this perfectly. The opening has a great shootout that sets the stage and shows you where the film is going. Midway through there is the scene where the bridge blows up, with the posse on horseback going into the river, and the film ends with a gigantic shootout, all expertly edited by Lou Lombardo.

Now, you are limited by what's in your film, but you should get the idea from this description of what kind of emotional balance a film needs, and you must address this as much as possible.

It is also important as to where you run your first cut. When I was a post supervisor at PM Entertainment in the 1990s, Joseph Mehri and Rick Peppin would run first cuts on the Avid. They would get phone calls during the running and stop to take them. I don't know how they could immerse themselves in the film that way.

When I was cutting for Sharon Blumenthal on the Women's Series for Showtime and Playboy, we were delivering short shows of about twenty-four minutes for a half-hour time slot. After finishing our cut, we brought a tape of it to the producers. The minute we started to run it, many of them would lower their heads and start making notes.

Sharon and I looked at each other in wonder. They weren't watching the movie. They were absorbed in making notes. The shows were only twenty-four minutes. They could have watched the show through once uninterrupted and then a second time to make notes. How much better would that be?

I edited several small features for Steven Paul at Crystal Sky Productions, and I developed a way of handling this. When the producers and executives came into the screening room, I handed them a continuity of the film. That's a list of every scene on every reel and how long each one runs and where it begins and ends in the reel. I would always hold the screening at 4:00 p.m. so that it was more or less the last event of the day.

I would tell the viewers to please concentrate on watching the film and hopefully enjoying it. I said that I did not want to discuss the film after the screening. I told them to take the continuity and go home and reflect on what they saw. In the morning they could make a list of notes that they felt should be addressed. Then I would make changes.

They beauty of this was that they were, like Orson Welles, watching the film as an audience and focusing on the material. Looking at it on the big screen, like God and DeMille intended, gave them a true perspective for making judgments. This is not possible on the Avid, the Moviola, or the KEM.

When I was cutting *Hail Caesar* for Anthony Michael Hall, I managed to keep him away from the film while I completed my first cut. It was his first directing job, and he was eager to see what was happening. He would often come by the cutting room, usually with a beautiful starlet in tow, hoping to get a glimpse of his epic.

One day he showed up with Sandra Bullock, before she was well known. He introduced me, and I could tell that he was dying to see something. I relented and called the screening room and asked if they could put up a reel for my director. They weren't busy and said that they could. I, of course, picked the best reel of the cut, and it was a good one, in which Michael appeared. I led them to the room and had them sit down to look at a forty-foot screen. I gave the reel to the projectionist.

The lights went down, and the reel began. I might as well have blown Michael and Sandra through the back wall. Michael was overwhelmed by what he saw. I went up to him and said, "Michael, don't ever make an editing decision outside of this room." Michael is a very smart man, and I guess he got it, because after running the entire first cut later in the month, he asked me to book the room the next day so that he could see the film again and make notes. After that we went back and began working on his cut in the editing room.

Chapter 8

Breaking the Sound Barrier

After the invention of the Moviola, film editing really took off. The ability to see what you were doing and to "audition" cuts before committing to them elevated patchers into film editors.

As previously stated, some editors rejected the Moviola because of running nitrate film over a heat source, but something was about to happen that changed everything. That was the advent of sound. Almost from the beginning, filmmakers had wanted to add sound to their films. Actually, silent movies were not silent. In larger theaters a live orchestra would accompany the film with a prepared score written for the film.

In smaller theaters, the score would be played on a phonograph record. So, silent audiences were accustomed to hearing as well as seeing. In 1926 Warner Brothers released *Don Juan*, starring John Barrymore, with sound effects and music accompanying the film on a record. All that was lacking was dialogue. That would follow in 1927 with *The Jazz Singer*. It had actual dialogue sequences, again on a record that ran in sync with the film.

Sound sent shockwaves through Hollywood. Suddenly, it was all-important for movies to talk. Stages had to be soundproofed for recording, and during actual shooting the camera had to be in a soundproof booth, with shooting done through a glass window. This was because the film running through a camera made a noise roughly corresponding to a saw mill in action. This, of course, inhibited camera movement.

There are those who say that creative filmmaking died with the coming of sound. Since the art form's beginnings at the turn of the twentieth century, filmmakers had learned to use the camera creatively to tell a story. Moving shots were common, and the camera was the chief instrument of moviemaking. Now, with the coming of sound, the camera was a prisoner to recording.

In an industry panicked by change, the sound recordist was a god on the set. His word was law. Microphones had to be positioned to record the spoken word, and films went back to the level of photographed stage plays because of these restrictions. This had to change.

Filmmakers began to learn that these restrictions applied only to dialogue scenes. A chase, a fight, or any action scene could be shot as before, and sound effects could be created separately and then cut in. In the early days of sound at Universal Pictures, an editor named Jack Foley came up with the system that still bears his name.

The edited film could be projected on a soundstage, and a Foley artist could record the various sounds to the picture as it was running. If a man was walking on cement, the artist could match his footsteps on a piece of cement on the stage, which could be recorded to the picture. Then, later in the editing room, any delays in sync could be adjusted in editing.

Looping was also invented. If dialogue recorded on the set was problematic, it could be replaced. The editor would create three loops. One would be the picture of the actor saying the line. A second loop would be the line itself, and a third loop would be sound with nothing recorded on it. The actor could watch himself saying the line as the loop went around and around. He would hear his original reading through headphones in sync with the picture. When he was ready, he could record a new reading on the third loop. Then the new line could be cut in to replace the old one.

I have heard that when Cecil B. DeMille went to make his first talking picture, he wanted to move the camera out of the booth to get a better angle. He was told by the soundman that this could not be done because of the noise from the camera. "Put a blanket around it," DeMille ordered. That was the beginning of the Barney and the sound blimp for cameras.

The sound blimp went around the camera, and when it was closed, you could not hear the camera. The operator had to look through a lens piece that provided a parallax view of what the camera was seeing. It wasn't through the camera lens, but it worked.

Because of sound, film stabilized at the rate of 24 frames per second (fps). This seemed to work best for picture and sound. Cranked cameras ran at the speed of the cameraman's cranking. When projected, film was at the mercy of the projectionist's cranking. Motors stabilized this, but various frame rates were tried. Sound made 24fps the established standard.

The early "talkies" projected in sync to a record that produced the sound. This caused sync issues when the record and picture weren't lining up. In Hollywood at the Pacific Theatre, when a big truck went past, the vibrations from it would cause the record to go out of sync. This was a very flawed system, and a way of putting the soundtrack on film had to be devised.

The problem was this: film runs intermittently, and sound has to be constant. In a projector a frame is pulled down and shown for less than one twenty-fourth of a second. Then a second frame is pulled down and shown. While it is being pulled down, a shutter goes in front of the projection lamp, and you do not see the frame being pulled down. Because of persistence of vision, the brain tends to see an object slightly longer than the eye is recording it. Therefore, a series of stills projected at 24fps appears to have motion.

This is the same as eye blinks. Because of persistence of vision, you are unaware that your eyes are blinking unless you think about it. You see what is going on around you without any awareness of the blinking.

If sound were placed on a film next to the frame being projected, it would not work. Someone, however, came up with a solution. Why not advance the sound of the frame being shown twenty frames? In doing so, a loop could be created below the projection lamp, and the sound reader could be in position at the end of the loop. The loop was the "Latham loop" from cameras, and it allowed the picture to be intermittent, while twenty frames ahead the sound could run at a constant speed. The loop kept the film from breaking and allowed two types of motion to occur at the same time. This solved the problem, and films were now going to stay in sync.

So, we have sound, but what good is it? Two filmmakers came along that put it to good use. One was Alfred Hitchcock. In his first sound film, *Blackmail*, he used it to advance the story. In an early scene a woman is lured to an artist's apartment, where he tries to take advantage of her. She ends up killing him with a knife. She hurries back to her apartment and pretends that she spent her night there.

Later, at breakfast, she is among the apartment dwellers who are discussing the murder, and the word "knife" is repeated over and over. Hitchcock uses the sound to emphasize the word. It so startles the young woman, who is cutting bread, that she drops the knife. Right away Hitchcock saw that he had a new tool for heightening suspense.

The other filmmaker to capitalize on sound was Orson Welles. For him it was natural because he had come directly from radio. Using sound was what radio was all about, and Welles was the master of it. In *Citizen Kane*, when the servant is describing how the second Mrs. Kane walked out there is a cut to a cockatoo screaming in the next cut. It adds tension to the scene and underscores what is happening.

Figure 8.1. Sound as a new tool in BLACKMAIL (1929), Alfred Hitchcock.

Figure 8.2. Welles' use of sound enhanced story in
CITIZEN KANE (1941), RKO Radio Pictures.

It wasn't long after the incorporation of sound that the use of color began to
develop. In the silent era, moods had been created by tinting film. Also, Technicolor
had developed a two-strip color system. In it two negatives were exposed in the same
camera. Each strip had a piece of the color information. When the two were printed
together, a color image was formed. It wasn't that good, but it was color. It was featured
in the 1933 film *The Mystery of the Wax Museum*, starring Fay Wray.

In 1935, *Becky Sharpe* became the first feature made in Technicolor's three-strip color
system. In the camera three negatives were exposed: yellow, cyan, and magenta. Printed
together, they created an accurate color picture. This was used in David O'Selznick's
Gone with the Wind. This type of system made color films expensive and difficult to
shoot, requiring a great deal of lighting.

When Selznick staged the burning of Atlanta, he had to shoot it on a Saturday so
that he could borrow every Technicolor camera in Hollywood. When editing, only one
strip was printed as work print so that the full effect of the color was not seen until
the film was finished. Every day the lab would print one roll in color to make sure that
everything was all right.

It wasn't until the end of the 1940s that color could be shot on a single strip of film.
This was done by having three layers of emulsion on the film: red, green, and blue. This
made it less expensive to shoot color, and color films took off. The Technicolor three-
strip process hung around until 1975. The last film shot in it was *Godfather II*. After that
the process was sold to China.

Toward the end of the twentieth century, Technicolor was working on reviving the
old system, but with the explosion of digital technology, it was too late. The parade had
already gone by.

Chapter 9

Cutting Room Etiquette

*I*t is time to speak of assistant editors and cutting room etiquette. Assistant editors are future editors. The best way to learn editing is to hang around a great editor. Many of Michael Kahn and Dede Allen's assistants have gone on to become great editors in their own right. Editing is a lot like a social disease. If you hang out with someone who has it, you'll pick it up eventually.

My friend Herb Dow, ACE, is fond of saying that he learned editing by sexual transmission. He married an editor's daughter. I'm not sure that he is far off the mark. Just being with editors on a daily basis, even if they don't specifically teach you anything, will give you skills for when you take command of a film.

Traditionally, the way to being an editor was this: you started in the Studio Shipping Department. On a lot, when you have a screening, you don't take the film yourself to the screening room. You call shipping, and they send a kid with a cart to pick up your film and move it. Afterward they return it to the cutting room.

During dailies, when things are hectic, an assistant will call Shipping and ask for a kid to help. When the kid arrives, he's given a task to do—usually mark picture or pop track. Marking picture consists of rolling down the incoming work print and marking the spot where the clapper on the slate closes. The scene and take are written on the film with a white marker.

Popping track consists of running down the incoming mag track, wearing head-phones, and indicating with a black marker exactly where the sound of the clapper comes together. Again, the scene and take number are written on the track. Individual takes are broken out and placed in a rack for syncing and building. Usually the first assistant does the actual building and syncing.

If the kid from shipping is smart, he learns these tasks well. Then he is asked back when help is needed. After a while he becomes the permanent apprentice in a cutting room. Over time that leads to becoming second and, eventually, first assistant. The

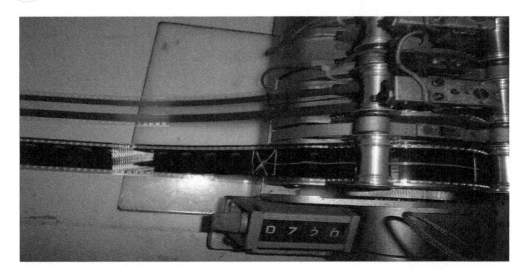

Figure 9.1. Picture and track marked and synced.

union rule used to be that you had to serve eight years as an assistant before you were allowed to edit. Eventually it was revised to five years, and now I don't think that there is a time element.

The eight-year rule was not such a bad thing. After serving eight years under different editors, the assistant really knew what he was doing. Also, he had made many contacts, and he was known. In the film business that is the most important thing: being known. When I came to Paramount Pictures in 1980 to start on *Shogun*, I was a complete unknown. I had come out of the Air Force, had worked on independents, and didn't know anyone. All of that worked against me.

All of this came apart with the Digital Revolution. With the advent of the Avid and Lightworks, many seasoned editors panicked. They weren't computer literate, and they were desperate to hold on to their jobs. They dropped many veteran assistants and grabbed less experienced and computer-literate assistants. We ended up with editors and assistants who came from two different worlds and sometimes didn't speak the same language.

It has gotten better in that some of the "old dogs" learned new tricks and began to understand Avid and Lightworks. Nevertheless, there has been a breach in a system that worked well for many years. We are learning to adapt to this.

When I was running post at PM Entertainment, we hired a young man with vast computer experience. I asked him, "What do you know about editing?" He proceeded to tell me about all the editing systems he was familiar with, which were extensive. I repeated the question.

"What do you know about editing?"

He thought a moment and replied, "Not much."

I said, "That's good. You can learn." And he did.

The editing room is the editor's personal fiefdom. He is in command, and the assistants are there to help him. There is a rule that applies here: an assistant should be seen and not heard; the editing room is not a democracy. Assistants should not speak unless spoken to. If they want to say something, they need to go through the editor.

I had a problem with an assistant at PM. She was a recovering attorney and used to saying things out loud and voicing her opinion. Her editor asked me to speak to her. I did. I made it clear to her that her job did not involve giving unsolicited opinions. If she did it again, I would fire her. She learned her lesson.

Editor Eric Sears, ACE, was in his cutting room one day when an apprentice told him that he thought that his editing of the picture was good. Eric turned slowly to him and asked him, "When did you see the picture?" The apprentice said that the assistants had run it the previous night while they were working.

Eric called his entire crew into his room and asked them why he shouldn't fire them. He explained that they had no right to be looking at the picture without permission. We work in a sensitive business, and idle chatter can lead to someone getting fired. It is important that assistants understand their boundaries and not cross them.

The editing room is a team. I protect my assistants, and I expect undying loyalty from them. Once, on a feature, the producer told me that he was going to fire my second assistant for reasons that had nothing to do with the picture. I told him that if he did that, the entire editing department would walk, and he could take the picture and stick it. He yelled at me and hung up. The next day he called and said, "I hate you, but let's get on with the editing." The second stayed.

When I was at Paramount, Paul Haggar, vice president of post-production, called my assistant John Hanson into his office. John returned to the cutting room and told me that he had been chewed out. I jumped on the phone and called Paul and yelled, "How dare you chew out my assistant? I'm coming over." I slammed down my phone and ran across the lot.

Fortunately I tried cutting through a stage and got lost. This gave me some time to calm down and I was not as crazed as I reached the Post Production building.

Paul's assistants ushered me in right away. "You're here to defend your friend," Paul cried.

I don't know where the words came from, but I yelled out, "I have no friends in the cutting room."

"I'm glad you said that," Paul replied.

My words calmed him down and we were both able to talk. I explained to him that if he had a problem with my assistant, he should come to me, and we would chew him out together. That defused the situation, and John was not bothered again.

Chapter 10

On the Waterfront: Helping the Actor's Arc through Editing

I n 1954, Columbia Pictures released On the *Waterfront*, directed by Elia Kazan and produced by Sam Spiegel. It starred Marlon Brando in the role that would earn him his first Academy Award. Brando plays Terry Malloy, an ex-fighter who runs errands for the mob that controls the longshoremen's union on the New York docks. The story was suggested by a series of articles by Malcolm Johnson about how a priest busted the mob in Boston that controlled the waterfront. Budd Schulberg wrote the screenplay from an original story of his own.

The strength of the film is in the character arc of Terry Malloy from mob stooge to a man who stands up against them. He is part of the "deaf and dumb" code of the waterfront. The part is well written, and Brando gives what is probably the finest performance of his career. It is exciting to watch, and the reality is flawlessly supported by Gene Milford's sensitive editing.

Film editing is storytelling, and to tell a story well you have to set it up properly. With this film you have a gifted screenwriter at the height of his powers. You have a director who has brought together an inspired group of actors who bring reality to the parts they play. It is the editor's job to pick the moments and the order to maximize the dramatic potential of the material and to bring into conflict the elements of the story. Gene Milford, inspired by the material given him, has done this throughout the movie.

The film opens with simple titles enhanced by a moody score from Leonard Bernstein. It was the only score he wrote specifically for a movie. As the first image comes on the screen, the score becomes powerful and energetic as we are introduced to Terry Malloy and the mob characters. Malloy is sent on an errand to lure Joey Doyle to his death. When he realizes what he has been duped into doing, his introspection into his life and the consequences of it begins.

Terry begins spending time with Doyle's sister Edie, but he is haunted by the guilt of having set Joey up. Finally, after confessing to Father Barry, he is told he has to tell

Edie what he did. The confession to Edie is emphasized by drowning out the dialog, and the scene is played totally with their reactions in large close-ups ending, with a wide shot as she runs away in horror. The lack of dialog raises the emotional level much higher than any words could. This leads to his "ratting out" Johnny Friendly and the mob before a crime commission.

Figure 10.1. The drowned-out confession.

After this, Terry is totally alienated. Both sides, the longshoremen and the mob, consider him a "stool pigeon," a traitor, and he has no friends. Even Tommy, a young man Malloy has been mentoring, teaching him boxing and raising homing pigeons, turns on him and kills all the pigeons in Malloy's coop. At this point, Terry decides to go down to the docks to claim what is his and have it out with Johnny Friendly.

The scene opens with wide shots as Malloy walks onto the docks and lines up for the work assignments. The longshoremen keep their distance. They give him the cold shoulder as Big Mac calls out the names of the men who are to work. As this happens, the scene cuts to the boat house where the mob sits plotting to kill Malloy, and Johnny Friendly tells his men that Terry "is mine! He's mine!"

Mac continues calling men and ignoring Terry. After everyone is called except Malloy, Mac says, "You want more of the same. Come back tomorrow." The longshoremen wait to see what Terry will do. Back in the boat house, Johnny Friendly collects his men's guns and puts them in the safe as he says, "We're a law-abiding union. Understand?" Terry starts to walk towards the boat house and the longshoremen follow.

Malloy calls out to Friendly and chucks a rock at the door. Friendly comes out and yells, "You think you're a big man because you can give the answers." Terry tells him, "You're a cheap, lousy, stinkin' mug, and I'm glad what I done to you!" Friendly goads him into a fight, and when Malloy starts to win, Friendly calls for his henchmen. They jump in and beat Terry senseless.

Father Barry and Edie show up and Friendly cries, "You want him? The little rat is yours!" They find Terry beaten and try to clean him up. At this point, the ship owner arrives and asks, "Who's in charge here? We gotta get this ship unloaded." Friendly cries, "I'm in charge. I'll get these men working." The longshoremen refuse to work without Terry. "Work? He can't even walk," Friendly exclaims. "You want to know who works? The guys I pick work!"

Friendly starts pushing the men, and an older longshoreman says, "All my life you've pushed me around." As Friendly grabs the man, he gets pushed off the pier and into the water. The longshoremen laugh, and it's the beginning of the breaking of Friendly's power. They tell the badly beaten Malloy that if he walks in to work, they will walk in with him.

Figure 10.2. The beaten Terry walks to victory.

Father Barry tells Terry, "You lost the battle, but you have a chance to win the war." Helping Terry onto his feet, he encourages the beaten man to stand up and try to lead the men in. Malloy staggers onto the wharf and makes his way to the open door to the work place. He arrives, and the ship owner says, "Okay. Let's go to work." The men proceed to follow Terry, ignoring Friendly who is trying to stop them—indicating his power is completely broken.

The many shots for this scene are arranged in a cohesive manner that builds the audience's emotions to the final moment. The editor has to be emotionally engaged with the material to bring this about. He or she must be one with the picture.

Filmmaking is a collaborative medium. This is both its strength and its weakness. No one person made *On the Waterfront* a great movie. It is all the artists collaborating together that achieved this. The famous contender scene between Marlon Brando and Rod Steiger in the back of the cab works so well because you have two artists playing off each other. For the whole movie it has to be that way, and it is the director's job to see that all the artists are making the same movie.

This is the most important thing a director does. Anyone can call "Action" and "Cut." Anyone can say, "Do it again." The real trick is to get everyone on board and moving in the same direction. That's what good directing is. If the directing is good, it naturally follows that the editing should be good, because the editor is similarly inspired and the footage leads him in the right direction.

Kazan said that in the contender scene he simply called action and let the two of them go. But both performers were making the same film as they took from each other. And Milford, as he pieced together the three angles of that scene while searching for the truth in every moment, was also making the same movie. Done properly like this is how an idea forms a script, is performed, and is shaped into the final piece that it is capable of being. This is what God and DeMille intended.

Chapter 11

Working with the Director

When you have shown your first cut, the real work begins. You have been working alone, and now you have a partner in the editing room: the director. You were single, and now you are married. There is that period of adjustment, in which you learn to live with each other. If it's your first project together, it may take a while to reach a good working relationship.

Some directors are content to come in and run a reel with you and give notes. They may want to look at other takes and discuss other approaches, but after giving instruction they are willing to leave you to work it out alone.

Other directors might actually want to set with you and frame fuck their way through the picture, being part of every decision. I have had it both ways, and the former is definitely the best way to go.

When I first had the good fortune of meeting director Robert Wise, I asked him about editing *Citizen Kane* with Orson Welles. As previously stated, he told me that Welles only saw the film in screening rooms and gave notes. As I explained, it was a good way to work, because Welles was always the audience and never involved himself in the minutiae of the editing process.

When I worked with Dan Curtis on *The Winds of War*, our routine was varied. Sometimes he was content to give me notes on what to do, and sometimes he wanted to go cut by cut with me. Mostly he was concerned with large action scenes, and he was happy enough with how I handled the drama. I did get a bit of a shock when he first came in the editing room.

Dan had just finished fourteen months of shooting on the project. I told him that I had the first show (three hours) together and asked whether he would like me to book a screening room so that we could run it. He said, "No," and I asked why.

He replied, "If you show me your cut on the screen, I will probably fire you. I have cut this in my mind, and I see it a certain way. I want to go through the picture reel by reel on the Moviola. Then, after making my changes, we can run it."

I had my heart set on running it on the big screen so that we could get a sense of the flow of the picture, but Dan was the director, and we would do it his way. So, we put up the first reel and started going through it. His changes were good, but not overwhelming. Pretty much we were on the same page about things.

Prior to starting the film, I had the studio supply me with every movie and TV movie that Dan had made. I watched them all with a hope of getting a sense of his style. I liked them and felt that Dan was a very creative director.

As Dan and I continued through the reels, things were going well. Then we came to the sequence that involved the strafing of the Polish column. It was September 1, 1939, the first day of the German invasion of Poland. Our main characters, Byron (Jan Michael Vincent) and Natalie (Ali McGraw), were escaping the advancing German army with a column of refugees when they were attacked by a German plane. Because it was an action sequence, it was covered by several cameras, and we had about forty thousand feet of film. That's approximately the equivalent of four two-hour movies.

I had labored for three weeks, going through footage and constructing a sequence that I felt played pretty well. I had the stunts, and the whole thing had a feeling of what it might really have been like. Dan watched it on the Moviola intently. At the end he said, "You've done a really great job with this." He paused and continued, "Now put it back into dailies, and we'll start over." I was horrified.

Fortunately, I had been warned by a former editor of Dan's that this might happen on an action sequence, and he had told me what to do. "OK, Dan," I said, "but before that, let's make a black-and-white dupe of the scene for protection." He agreed, and it was decided that we would get together in a couple of days, when everything was back in dailies. I immediately sent the work print of the scene off to a lab to make the black-and-white duplicate copy. Afterward the team of assistants rushed to take the scene apart and put it back into dailies.

Dan, John Hanson, and I assembled two days later on the KEM flatbed editing machine to view the raw footage. As we proceeded, Dan would call a halt when he saw a shot that he wanted, and I would pull it. I told Dan to describe the shot and John to write the description down on a legal pad. The shot was numbered and hung in a trim bin. We then continued to the next shot.

Interestingly, when we pulled shots, I would usually discover a splice, indicating that it was a shot that I had pulled before for my cut of the sequence. We continued until we had one hundred shots pulled and hanging in trim bins along the wall of Cutting Building One on the Paramount Pictures lot. Incidentally, it's the same building in which Robert Wise had cut *Citizen Kane* when it had been part of the RKO Pictures Studio.

Dan wanted to start cutting immediately, but I convinced him to wait while I made a catalog of the shots we pulled. Because this was before computers, we began xeroxing

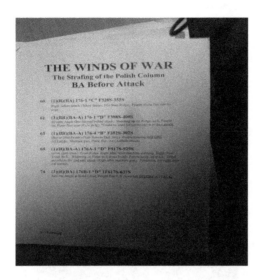

Figure 11.1. Reproduction of the catalog for cutting action scene in THE WINDS OF WAR (1982), Paramount Pictures.

John's notes and cutting them up so that we could arrange the shots in the order of the sequence. When Dan came into the cutting room, I handed him a catalog.

Dan declared, "OK. Let's start with the shot of—"

"Hold on," I interjected. "Point to the shot you mean in the catalog. Give us a number."

Dan began reading his catalog. "Shot 66," he said. "That's the one."

"Go get it," I told John. He immediately streaked down the hall and returned with shot 66. I took it and jammed it into the Moviola. "No! No!" Dan yelled. "That's not the one." He gazed at the catalog again and called out another number. John took 66 back and returned with the new shot. This time it was right.

That's how we did Dan's cut of the strafing of the Polish column. Sometimes we would get stuck, and I would say, "Let's look at what Jack did." We would put up the black-and-white dupe of my version and look at it. "That's it! That's how to do it," Dan would cry. So at that point we would go back to what I had before. We continued for a month. At the end of that time, we had a version that closely resembled mine, but with Dan's touches.

It was not how I had wanted to work, but it did work, and Dan got to have his hand on the scene. Other scenes, particularly dialogue and love scenes, he would pass with only a few changes. When we had gone through the whole three hours, we ran the film on the big screen, and Dan was happy.

When I worked with Larry Peerce on *The Fifth Missile*, because I had never even met him, I did research on his old films. I ran *Goodbye Columbus*; *The Incident*; *One Potato, Two Potato*; *The Other Side of the Mountain*; *Two-Minute Warning*; and *The Bell Jar* before leaving for Cinecitta Studios in Rome, Italy. I met Larry the first day of shooting on the

Figure 11.2. Author with Director Larry
Peerce in Rome, Italy.

set. I suggested that he come in and look at what I was putting together in a couple of days. He did, and even gave me notes, and we both saw that we were on the same page.

After that Larry didn't look at any cutting until Maureen O'Connell, my coeditor, and I ran the picture for him and producer Eric Bercovici. After seeing the film, both of them came into the editing room, and we ran the reels on the Prevost flatbed editing machine. They jointly gave me notes and left me and Maureen to make the appropriate changes. Editing with Eric and Larry was a very pleasant experience. There was no ego, and we all were able to work creatively, with no big fights.

Most directors I have worked with have given me a positive experience. Some spent more time with me than others, but that depended on their other commitments. Ideally, this moment should be a collaboration between artists for the good of the picture.

Early on I learned that you tell a director something once. If he doesn't want to hear it or try it, you move on and never bring it up again. He is the team leader, and it's his picture. If an editor and a director don't get along, they shouldn't be working together. One of them has to go, and usually it's the editor.

Directors do not have an easy job. They're expected to know everything, and, of course, they don't. Our job is to nurture them and make them feel secure while helping guide them toward making the best movie possible. Sure, the director will get the lion's share of the credit, but we as editors know what we did. If we wanted more, we would have been directors.

And maybe some of us should be. We are known as the second director of the picture. Usually on successful television shows, an editor will be offered the chance to direct an episode as a carrot to keep him on board. It's a natural progression, because the editor knows what coverage is needed. Because the show is a series, he doesn't have to discuss character much with the regulars. All he has to do is tell them where to stand and keep things moving. The guest cast may need a little help, but that's not so overwhelming.

A good editor has a sense of pacing that helps in directing. Of course, he needs to be able to deal with people and manipulate them. He needs to have a vision for the project and be able to communicate it to his cast and crew. You are dealing with sensitive, creative people with egos.

I have always felt that editors are the real assistant directors. The ones on the set are really assistant production managers. They schedule shooting, manage the paperwork, and keep track of the talent. This usually leads to their becoming production managers. From editing, it is a natural step into directing.

I was told that the directors originally asked us to join their guild instead of the International Alliance of Theatrical and Stage Employees. We made the mistake of going with the IA and became just another craft under that umbrella. When I worked for the *Cinemaeditor*, I wrote an editorial suggesting that we should pull out of the IA and go with the DGA. The IA was not happy and made it known to me.

As it happens, many of the editors in the American Cinema Editors hold both a union card for film editing and a DGA card for directing. It is two sides of the same coin.

Chapter 12   *The Winds of War Saga*

H aving spent six months on the feature version of Shogun, I felt my career was really taking off. After seventeen years in low-budget work, I was on the Paramount lot working on material that would be seen by everyone. I had noticed that Dan Curtis had taken over the old Lucille Ball building and was preparing a miniseries version of Herman Wouk's novel *The Winds of War*. I had recently read the book and was excited at the possibility of perhaps working on it.

I had no connections to Dan Curtis, so I could not think how to approach him. I knew he had created the *Dark Shadows* television series and had done a number of movies-of-the-week. Bernie Gribble, ACE, was his editor, but he had departed the project to do a feature so Dan was without an editor.

After finishing *Shogun*, I had been given a week on a behind-the-scenes for the film. The project got cancelled, but for one week we were in business. My friend Kerry Feltham was to direct it, and Don Silverman was producing for the studio with Judee Gustafson as the associate producer. I had first met Judee on *Shogun* when I needed an additional assistant to help me in cutting a promo. I already had Maureen O'Connell, but we were on a time crunch and extra hands were needed. She was sent over from shipping, where assistants got their start.

I was stunned when she walked in. She was beautiful and truly looked like a Las Vegas showgirl. My immediate thought was, "This is what an assistant looks like. Can I get two?" For the documentary, some of the other people involved did not respect Judee because they knew she came out of the shipping department. I took her part and said to them, "The studio made her the associate producer, and that's the end of it. I do what she says."

While I was trying to figure how to approach Dan Curtis, I discovered that Judee was still working with Don Silverman, who was attached to *Winds* as an associate producer. I thought this might be my connection, so I asked Judee to have lunch with me off the lot.

In accepting my invitation to lunch, Judee had no idea what I wanted. Because she was such a beautiful woman I thought she might think I was going to hit on her. I drove us to Au Petit Café over at Vine and La Mirada where I had an account and could sign for lunch. We were seated in a small booth in the exclusive basement section. It was perfect for a romantic meal. After drinks and ordering, I still had not indicated anything of my intentions and was enjoying keeping Judee in suspense.

Figure 12.1. Judee Gustafson with Jack Tucker.

Eventually, I decided to come right to the point. "I want to edit *Winds of War*, and I need you to get me an interview with Dan Curtis." I don't know if Judee was relieved or not with my request, but she indicated she could do this. "I'll get you an interview," she said. I did not realize what a friend Judee would turn out to be.

A few weeks went by, and the head of television post called me and said I had a meeting with Dan Curtis. "Don't say I never did anything for you," he said. He had no idea that Judee was working behind the scenes as he took the credit due to her.

When I met Dan Curtis, he was surprised to learn that I had actually read the book *The Winds of War*. I asked him how he was going to film certain scenes, and he would tell me. "How are you going to do this?" I asked. In the novel, Herman Woulk had included sequences that were supposedly from a textbook by a German General Von Roon. These little interruptions to the story helped explain what certain things meant.

Robert Graves, who had written *I, Claudius*, had been hired to adapt *Winds* as a screenplay. Since we couldn't interrupt our screenplay with General Von Roon's textbook, Graves decided to create Von Roon as an actual character in the story. Jeremy Kemp was eventually hired to play the part. In this way, Von Roon would interact with our main character, Pug Henry, and could clarify things.

Graves began working on the script and then unfortunately died. Herman Woulk himself then took over, following the outline Graves had created. He was able to complete the shooting script.

Dan explained this and much of what he had been prepping for over the past year. In my interview we seemed to get on well, but I was worried. I knew other editors were applying for the job. I went to Eric Bercovici, the producer of *Shogun*, and asked him to call Curtis on my behalf, which he did.

My big gun was James Clavell, author of *Shogun*. He had liked what I had done with the feature. "Mr. Clavell," I said, "You say you like what I did on your show. Will you tell that to Dan Curtis?" "Certainly," Clavell replied, reaching for the phone. He got Dan right away, but Dan didn't believe it was Clavell. The conversation went something like this:

"Hello, this is James Clavell."

"Who is this really?" Dan asked.

"This is James Clavell."

"C'mon. Don't put me on."

"I am James Clavell."

"No, you're not. You're my production manager trying to put one over on me."

Eventually Dan realized that he was indeed talking to James Clavell. Clavell then chimed in with, "Tucker's the one." He praised me for a few minutes and then went on to talk about the wonder of *Shogun* for the next half hour. Judee Gustafson told me later that if one more person called Dan about me, he was going to flip. Nevertheless, Dan hired me on what, at that time, was the most expensive television miniseries ever filmed.

Because I had never worked for Dan Curtis, I had Paramount provide me with tapes of as many of Dan's films as were available. I watched them in a video room and liked what I saw. I viewed *When Every Day Was the Fourth of July*, *The Long Days of Summer*, *Mrs. R's Daughter*, *Melvin Purvis, G-Man* and many others, trying to get a sense of who Dan Curtis was. I always do this with a new director, and I highly recommend it.

I wanted Maureen O'Connell to assist me as she had on *Shogun*, but Paul Haggar, the vice president of post-production, refused to pay her over scale. She was pissed and went off to follow Eric Bercovici to MGM, where he had two pilots going: *McClain's Law* and *The Chicago Story*. I turned to my former assistant Michael Knue, ACE, who had found me Maureen, and he suggested Ruth Bird.

I interviewed Ruth and was thrilled to learn that she had previously worked for Dan Curtis as an assistant to Bernie Gribble, ACE. I felt she could guide me in handling this very volatile director.

A week before production was scheduled to start, I had the production office put me and Ruth on salary, so we could prepare the cutting room for what was to come. I knew they were shooting for fourteen months in six countries on two continents. Production told me they were shipping a coding machine to Yugoslavia for the assistants over there to code the dailies. I thought, "Good luck trying to get a coding machine back out of a communist country."

The plan was that editorial would remain in Hollywood at Paramount. In each country that they were shooting in, local assistants would sync up the dailies, code them, and run them for Dan before shipping them to Hollywood. I was concerned about what coding system we should use when Ruth made an inspired suggestion. "They don't need to code them. All they need is to sync them up for viewing. We'll code them after they arrive at the studio."

So the coding machine that was shipped to Yugoslavia was useless for our purpose. Besides, in that country coding was done by hand, with the assistant writing the numbers on the film. Maybe the coding machine was some sort of bribe. I don't know, but it was never seen or heard of again.

I went over to the *Happy Days* set where I heard the director of photography, Steven Larner, was shooting smoke tests. To give the show a period look, smoke was added in some of the scenes. I introduced myself to Larner, who had shot *The Buddy Holly Story*, and watched the tests for a while.

We had a read-through of the script that took all day. A read-through is important because with the crew leaders assembled, everyone knows what their responsibilities are for a given scene. For editing, it's usually about playbacks on the set or stock footage. For some of the naval scenes we were going to be shooting blue screens, and we needed to do registration tests on the cameras.

Blue screens are scenes where actors are filmed before a blue screen. Optically, the blue can then be replaced by whatever background you want. It is important that you make sure that both shots have rock-steady registration, so they don't move against each other when combined. Today this process has been pretty much replaced with green screens.

The Winds of War scripted had approximately 1,800 scenes, so in the read-through it was slow going. I fell asleep as we plodded forward, and after lunch the production manager said I didn't have to attend because very little involved postproduction.

As production approached, casting was still trying to button down several parts. The main character, Pug Henry, was a part that physically fit Paul Newman. He wouldn't do it. The problem with getting an actor for the part was they had to commit to over a year. At the last minute, I heard that Robert Mitchum had agreed to play the part. I was delighted, having watched him in such films as *Cape Fear, Thunder Road,* and *The Night of the Hunter.*

I had recently watched Mitchum on a TV talk show where he was asked why he had never directed. Mitchum said, "If I directed, I would spend time in those little cutting rooms with the editors. They're a bunch of little albinos. They only let them out for lunch." I decided I would introduce myself to Mitchum as "the Albino from the Cutting Room."

On Monday, December 1, 1980, the cameras began to roll on *The Winds of War*. First setup was on the Queen Mary in Long Beach. It was doubling as the German liner *Bremen* that was taking Pug Henry (Robert Mitchum) and his wife (Polly Bergen) to Germany. As is my custom, I drove to the set to see how things were going.

I found the crew assembled on the top deck where Mitchum was doing a scene with Victoria Tennent, who had been just hired as Pamela Tudsbury, the young woman Pug begins to fall in love with. Barbara Steele, the associate producer, was talking to Mitchum, who announced that he was down here for "the raping season."

Mitchum terrified me. He was huge, as big as John Wayne. The idea of actually speaking to him was more than I could manage. I quietly watched as the actors performed their lines. I did speak with Barbara Steele, whom I had seen in the Italian horror movie *Black Sunday* and Roger Corman's *The Pit and the Pendulum*, as well as Federico Fellini's *8 ½*. I watched for a while and then headed back to Paramount to prepare for first day's dailies.

The first month on the shooting schedule was three weeks in Los Angeles before the Christmas break. Then it was on to Yugoslavia in January for three months, back to Hollywood for a month to regroup, and back to Europe. I met Larry Johnson, the script supervisor who had also done *Shogun*, so I was familiar with his work. He had done a complete timing of the show as to how long he felt scenes would cut to. He knew his business, and after editing three hours of the production, the difference in his timings and the actual cut was only seconds. He was the best script supervisor I ever worked with.

On Tuesday, December 2, we had our first dailies from the Queen Mary. Ruth expertly synced them up. Around 10:00 a.m. I ran them for the Paramount executives and then at 5:00 p.m. they went to ABC to view; they were back on the lot in time to run with Dan Curtis after he wrapped the days shooting. We might run with Dan at 10:00 p.m. or later.

When Dan arrived, I sat next to him to hear his feelings, and Ruth was next to me to take notes. Dan relaxed with a martini as we rolled the film in the screening room. I had the advantage of having seen the film already. Dan was pretty specific about what he liked or didn't like. One thing he told me was never to do a direct cut-in from a wide shot to a close-up. "Always cut to the other actor first. It makes a softer cut. Only do a direct cut-in for shock value." I listened to Dan's words and still use his theories of editing to this day.

On the third, I actually began cutting the scenes Dan had shot that first day on the Queen Mary. I cut a sequence I liked and set it aside to take on the next one. Dan did not immediately ask to see anything.

We began shooting in the Hancock Park neighborhood of Los Angeles. It was doubling for Berlin. As I recall, some writer had described L.A. as Berlin with palm trees. Dan began shooting all the sequences that involved the house. I watched the dailies as they came in with the executives and then in the evening with Dan.

One morning, Dan called me from the set.

"How are the dailies?" he asked.

"Fine. Everything looks good," I said.

"How's Mitchum?"

"He's okay. His performance is a little slow."

"Damn it! The son of a bitch was drunk."

That was my introduction to Mitchum's drinking. In watching his performances, I learned that Mitchum was a true professional. If there was a comma in the script, he paused. He knew every word perfectly, and he was prepared. When he drank he just performed slower, but he had every word down.

In shooting the sequences of the *Bremen* leaving New York, Dan had a trick to make it look like the Queen Mary was pulling out. He had actors standing on a dolly. That dolly moved in one direction while a second dolly with the camera went in another direction. It looked pretty good. For wider shots, I found stock footage of a liner leaving New York.

In regards to stock footage, we had Sue Breitrose as our film librarian and Stephanie Dubov as a researcher. Sue would spend many hours in Projection Room 13 above the cutting rooms, watching World War II movies seeking footage we could use. Sometimes I would join her. Most of the color films we saw looked pink because the vegetable dyes in the color had shifted over time. They were studio prints, and no one was going to make a new print.

After three weeks, we broke for Christmas. In January, the crew moved to Yugoslavia, and I continued working with the material I had. About three weeks later, we received our first shipment of dailies. It was about three hours of footage, synced but not coded. I ran with the executives and sent it to ABC. When it returned, Ruth coded it and broke it down for editing.

Before he left, Dan instructed me to cull the dailies before showing them. "Just show them enough that they can see I've covered the scene. Don't bury them in footage." So as footage came in, I ended up viewing on the KEM flatbed and pulling out extra footage. This took a lot of time, and I eventually asked Ruth to do this for me, so I had time to edit. By this time we'd picked up Gary Smith as another assistant and occasionally pulled people from shipping.

During this time, Larry Johnson started sending me notes as to what Dan liked or didn't like in dailies. While screening, Dan would speak, and Larry, realizing there was no one taking notes, started writing them down and sending them on to me. They were very helpful and often amusing. While he was in Europe, I had no direct communication with Dan, and I began to feel uneasy.

At this time Paul Haggar tried to interest me in leaving *Winds* for a feature. John Frankenheimer was preparing to shoot a show in Japan called *The Challenge*. "Wouldn't you like to go on location to Japan?" Paul asked. I replied, "No, I want to stick with *Winds*." He also tried to interest me in *The White Dog*, which was to be directed by the legendary Sam Fuller. I had an interview with Fuller, and his producer Jon Davison asked me if Paul was my agent. "He's really pushing you," he said. It was becoming obvious that Dan was going to fire me, and Paul was trying to protect the studio from me suing them.

When Dan returned three months later, he fired the whole crew from Steven Larner on down. I was included; only Larry Johnson and the gaffer were retained. Dan asked me to stay on until a new editor could be hired. I figured he'd get Bernie Gribble, ACE. He said, "This project means everything to me, and I can't work with anyone I'm not sure of." At this point Dan had not seen any of my work, and I thought he was being reactionary.

So, in the break from European shooting Dan started running footage with me. He liked what I had done but of course had changes for me, which I made. I began to think Dan was sorry he fired me and didn't know how to get out of it. Paul Haggar called me one night and told me not "to take any other job. "What does this mean?" I asked. "Just don't take anything. He wants you to stay," Haggar confided.

Now I had the upper hand. I knew Dan liked my work and wanted me to continue. As we were working one morning, Dan quietly said, "I like your editing. I want you to stay on the project."

"What was that, Dan? I didn't hear you."

Louder, Dan said, "I want you to stay on."

"I'm sorry, Dan. I can't hear what you're saying."

"I want you to stay," Dan yelled.

"What's that?"

Dan screamed to me, "I want you to stay."

I looked him in the eye and said, "Okay, but I want a raise."

"I'll see what I can do," Dan said.

We continued through the edited footage, making Dan's changes. Later Dan went over to talk to Paul Haggar about my raise. I was making scale, which at the time was about $1,050 and I was hoping to jump to $1,500. Dan called me later and said, "Your boss is really tough. The best I could get for you was another hundred dollars."

"It's okay, Dan. You went to bat for me. That's enough."

Dan went back to Europe. This time he had Charlie Correll, ASC, as his director of photography. One good thing to come out of the firings was Dan got to reshoot a scene where Mitchum and Victoria Tennent were talking in the snow in Russia. Originally, they just sat on a rock and talked. In the new version, it was a dolly shot as they walked by the Russian soldiers, and it looked great.

During this time, I started getting pay at the $1,500 level. I thought maybe Paul had a change of heart. It was not so, and I got a call from Paul to come over to his office.

"We've been overpaying you," Paul said. Apparently, Paul had written a note saying to add $150, and payroll interpreted it as $1,500. "Why didn't you tell us?"

"Dan said he'd get me a raise. This is a raise."

"I'm putting you down to $1,200, and you'll have to pay back the difference."

"I'm not paying it back. It's your mistake. You pay it back."

I realized that if I beat Haggar I would be making a powerful enemy. We needed a compromise. Paul suggested, "If you work eight Saturdays, that would make up the difference." I agreed to this.

Beginning that Saturday, I would drive to the studio and go to the cutting room. I would clock in around 10:00 a.m. and straighten up the room some. Then I would take a nap. Around noon I would go to my favorite restaurant for a liquid lunch. Then I would come back and sleep until about four when I would clock out. So, this way Paul got his eight Saturdays, and I didn't work them. It was a perfect compromise.

I had been on the picture for about a year now, and I wanted to take a vacation. I told Paul Haggar.

"You can't go on vacation. We're in production. I've never heard of such a thing as an editor taking a vacation while we're in production."

"This is an unusual film, Paul. We're shooting for fourteen months. Dan's in Europe and won't be back for several weeks."

"We'll close down the cutting room for a week."

"No, the assistants have plenty of work to do."

So, we agreed, I would take off a week, but my assistants would continue to work. A week later I came back much refreshed.

When Dan returned from Europe, he was angry. "What's wrong?" I asked. "That drunk is trying to ruin my movie." Dan was referring to a scene where Mitchum and Victoria were standing at the Thames river during a German blitz. Behind them were several buildings burning. It was a controlled burn from gas jets, but it was an expensive scene to shoot, probably the most expensive in the movie. As they stood

Figure 12.2. Victoria Tennent and Mitchum in the big scene.

there, Mitchum was supposed to say, "These fires have lighted the way for the German planes." What came out was very slurred.

Dan had me get all of that footage together on a reel, so he could run it for Mitchum. I did this and took it to a screening room. Dan and Mitchum went in. I stayed in the booth with the projectionist, so I have no idea what was happening in the screening room. The reel finished, and after a few minutes Dan and Mitchum walked out. They were both smiling. Mitchum said, "We'll drink on it."

During this last shoot in Europe, Lee Strasberg, the famous co-founder of the Actor's Studio in New York, had joined the cast playing Ali McGraw's uncle. I had received some of his footage, and his performance was uninspiring. I asked Dan if the man was sick or just getting old.

"No," Dan exclaimed. "He can't act."

"Dan, you're talking about an icon of American acting," I cried.

"He's a bad actor, Jack. We've got to get rid of him."

"I know how we can do it. I'll put together all of his takes like we did with Mitchum. I won't cull out anything. We'll send it all over to ABC. We'll bury him."

"Do it," Dan said. I did it, and Strasberg was fired. Now the question was who to replace him with. The vice president of Paramount Television, Gary Nardino, wanted Danny Kaye, and so did I. Dan would have none of it. He wanted John Houseman, and that's who we got. I personally thought Houseman was still playing his character from *The Paper Chase*, but he was a vast improvement over Strasberg.

Figure 12.3. Lee Strasberg with Ali McGraw before he was fired.

There was a sequence in the script concerning the Palio which was crucial to the story. The Palio is a race that is run in Sienna, Italy every year in July and August. The various neighborhoods of Sienna each have a horse in the race to see which is the best neighborhood. There are no rules, and jockeys can kick and hit each other; do anything they like to win. If a jockey is knocked from his horse, the horse can still win.

The people of Sienna spend a great deal of time and effort preparing the town square for this race, and it actually is over in about two minutes. The first Palio is run in July, and a second one is run in August. Dan had filmed the first race and certain things had to happen in the race to fit our story. I suggested to Dan we cut together the footage we had and figure out what he needed to shoot for the second Palio.

Obviously, we needed shots of Jan Michael Vincent, Ali McGraw, and the newly hired John Houseman watching the race and commenting. Then we needed close-ups of what they were reacting to, and all this cut into the race footage we had. Dan and I cut together what we had with the crowds and the race and inserted slugs of leader to indicate where the new shots would go. Then I had a tape made of it that Dan could refer to as he was shooting. Dan went back to Italy and picked up the necessary shots.

Figure 12.4. The Palio race.

In Dan's absence, I began editing on a sequence called Klovnow Station. In it, the neutrals are being evacuated from Warsaw, Poland, after the German invasion. When they reach Klovnow Station they are treated to a feast by the Germans. Afterwards, the Gestapo comes in to supervise their departure. They want to know if there are any Jews among the American evacuees. Leslie Slote, the American diplomat (David Dukes) is unwilling to give this information. It is a wonderful scene because Slote is essentially a coward and does not want to stand up to the Gestapo, but he can't bring himself to name the Jews. Dan got all the right shots. I cut it perfectly, and it is the best scene I ever cut.

When I showed the scene to Dan, he was thrilled. "I'm so glad that we cut this," he said.

"We?" I asked. "I cut this sequence on my own."

"It's not possible," Dan said. "Even if you had eight Academy Awards you could not have cut this by yourself. Not only do you always cut to the right shot, but you hold it for exactly the right amount of time."

This became an issue with us. Dan had been eating, drinking, and sleeping *Winds of War*, so he often dreamed of cutting scenes that hadn't been cut. On one occasion, I had to show him the dailies on a scene to prove they weren't cut. I was determined that he should know who he was talking to. I wanted him to know how good I was. Eventually, Ruth Bird and I convinced him that I had cut it alone. Then he made changes in the scene that was already perfect.

It's always a mistake to argue with a director. If you win, you lose. The director is the artistic team leader, and you need to go with his or her vision. I feel that by besting Dan with this sequence, I was creating a rift between us. But God bless it, I wanted him to know how good I was and maybe for thirty seconds he did. After that it was merely an attack on his ego, and a director needs his ego intact.

Shortly after this, I told Dan we needed to add another editor to the team. I told him I wanted to have some say in who we picked. I didn't get any. Dan brought in Bernie Gribble, ACE, who had finished editing *The White Dog*. Not only did he hire Bernie, but he moved him up to first editor. Paul Haggar had to explain this to me and calm me down so I didn't make a fuss with the union. It was a cute little trick, but they pulled it off.

I went to see Bernie and told him I was at his service. I said, "I'm told you are now in charge."

"Someone has to be in charge," he replied.

It was an awkward situation for both of us, but we both rose to the occasion. Bernie was a very talented editor, having edited *Death Wish* and *The Man in the White Suit*, and I came to value his friendship and experience. Other people on the show still turned to me for leadership.

Ruth Bird asked me one day if she could cut a scene. I told her, "Yes." It has always been my policy to encourage my assistants to cut. I feel they are editors-in-training and part of the editor's job is to teach them to cut. Besides, when you're under the gun they can help. I told Ruth that she could not take credit for cutting the scene until I had shown it to Dan and he had approved it. That way he would assume it was just something I did, and he would not approach it with any prejudice.

Ruth picked out a scene and went to work. She expertly shaped the material, and when it was finished I ran it for Dan.

"That scene was nicely cut," Dan volunteered.

"Ruth cut it," I explained.

"Really?"

"Yes, she knows her stuff."

Bernie felt we needed to pick up another editor, and Dan told us to show him some candidates. We looked at the Contract Services Availability Roster and picked a few editors we knew. Dan interviewed them but didn't like them. "They don't look like editors to me," he said. Bernie and I looked at each other. "What does an editor look like?" Bernie asked. "Like you and me," I replied.

Dan decided he wanted our assistant Gary Smith to be the third editor. He and Gary got along well together, but we wondered what Gary's editing experience was. At that time, the five-year rule was still in place and Gary had to serve another six months as an assistant before he could move up. We approached the Motion Picture Editor's Guild and explained that Gary was who Dan wanted, and he would wait six months if necessary to get him. The Guild waved the six months, and Gary was moved up.

Ruth Bird had wanted to move up, but Dan Curtis had told her in no uncertain terms that "no woman is going to cut my movie." I believe that Ruth threw an ash tray at Dan. She told Paul Haggar she was quitting the project and stormed off. I told Paul to disregard anything she said to him. I knew Ruth needed the job. She had a son to support.

Cecelia Hall and I went over to Ruth's house and approached her like two cops interrogating a suspect. Between us, we argued Ruth into staying on the show. There was no point in her losing her job over this. The next day, things were back to normal.

After being on the show for over a year, I finally got the chance to go on location. It wasn't Europe, but at least it was out of town. Dan decided he wanted me along for the Pearl Harbor/Cavite shoot. I was to spend four days at Point Hueneme, 50 miles from Hollywood, to be available with footage while Dan shot the attacks on those two bases. Not only was I to be there, but John Hansen and a cutting room were to be there.

We brought a KEM flatbed for viewing and a TV and tape deck, plus an editing bench, Moviola and editing equipment. We were to go up Thursday afternoon and run dailies for Dan. We brought a projector and a projectionist too. We were stopped at the Paramount gate because they thought we were stealing the TV. Paul Haggar had to clear us, and we were off to location.

We arrived at the hotel, and I saw a most unusual sight. I was born during World War II and as I grew up if someone saw me gazing off into space and asked what I was looking at I would say, "I'm watching for Japanese planes." At the hotel, I looked up and I finally saw Japanese planes circling overhead.

After getting assigned a room, I was driven to where they were shooting on the dock. I pulled up as a bomb went off and a stunt man came running out on fire. "Cut," yelled Dan Curtis perched up in the air on a crane overseeing the action. He immediately spotted me.

"Jack, how are my dailies?" Dan asked.

"They're fine," I replied.

"Only fine?"

"No, I mean they're fabulous. Some of the best I've ever seen." I was starting to catch on.

Dan descended from his godlike perch, and I told him we would set up at the hotel and he could see how truly great they were.

We set up in a building adjacent to the hotel, and that first night we watched the dailies we had brought with us. The pilots were there that were flying the planes that looked like Japanese Zeros. After dailies they would go over with Dan how they would fly the next day to get the shots that were needed. The KEM was placed in a room out on the wharf so Dan could see silent dailies as soon as they arrived.

The next morning when picture arrived from Hollywood, we threaded a roll up on the KEM and Dan sat down to watch it. He pushed the forward button on the machine, and the picture took off like a rocket. Condensation from the moisture in the air had gotten into the wiring and the KEM was uncontrollable. Quick-thinking John Hansen ran over to makeup and borrowed a hair dryer in a vain attempt to dry the wiring. Dan had to wait till the evening and see synced dailies on the projector.

Figure 12.5. Attack on Cavite Naval Base.

On the Paramount lot, I used to run into Peter Zinner, ACE. He kept talking about what a wonderful project *Winds* must be. I kept reminding him, "Peter, it's a TV show. You are a feature editor. You edited *The Godfather*. You don't want to be part of a TV show." Nevertheless, he persisted in his interest.

We went to a fourth editor with John Burnett, ACE. Dan told him how he wanted the editing done, and Burnett replied, "Let me tell you how I work. I cut the scene. You leave me alone. When I'm ready, I show it to you as I see it. After that, I'll change it any way you want, upside down and sideways." Burnett was hired.

We finished principal photography in December, and on the last day I went to the set in the Larchmont District. When the crew saw me, they became worried. Previously my visits were because someone had made a mistake. I assured them, "There's nothing wrong. I'm just here to see Ali McGraw."

In January, we moved into the "B" tank on the lot. All studios used to have a "B" tank, and Paramount had the last one in Hollywood. These were tanks where you could shoot water scenes, usually with model ships. Currently the tank was used as part of the parking for the studio. I had asked to have it filled so we could run tests, but since it cost $60,000 to fill the tank and we would lose part of the parking lot, we had no tests. The tests would be as we shot as part of the production.

Charlie Correll, ASC, advised Dan to hire Jack Cooperman, ASC, to shoot the footage, as he was a specialist in this type of photography. Cooperman took charge of the

Figure 12.6. The convoy scene in the "B" tank.

unit, and we began shooting. Mostly we shot the model ships for the convey sequence. The ships were connected to cables and then winched across the tank. Equipment was brought in to pound the water to create waves. The film was shot at 120fps instead of 24fps to slow down and smooth out the action. Dan decided for expedience to have a dressing room set up with a KEM viewing machine inside. Then as dailies came in, I could cut it into a sequence to see how well it worked.

Each day Dan would climb into a pair of waders and join the crew in the tank setting up the shots. We had a video tap connected to give an idea what was being recorded. When dailies came in, we would view them in the screening room, and then I would cut them into the proper sequence and Dan would approve or disapprove the shot.

We were in the tank for 30 days. Film was exposed, and Dan would see if it worked. Soon we learned that the waves worked best right after the wave pounders were turned off. Besides the convoy, we shot a couple of takes of Pearl Harbor after the attack as well as the last shot of the film with Mitchum watching the aircraft carrier *Enterprise* heading out to sea. We wrapped the tank and shooting on *Winds* was over.

Figure 12.7. The "B" tank with the studio in the background. The studio was blocked out and replaced with a shot prepared by the special effects department.

Figure 12.8. Author in front of the "B" tank for Pearl Harbor.

During this time, Gary Smith was having a problem with his assistant who thought he was a better editor than Gary. I was still looked to for leadership, so I called them both into my room. Gary's assistant tried to make a case that he should be editing and not Gary.

I said, "I don't care how good an editor you are. I hired you to assist Gary Smith. If you can't do that, I'll fire you and get someone who can. Gary is the editor. There's nothing to discuss." That ended it, and the assistant behaved.

At this time, it occurred to me that American television was going to go stereo. Japan already had it, and it seemed to me *Winds of War* was the perfect show to introduce it to the American public. Stereo was not available in the United States, but there were stereo simulcasts. Mostly it was used for concerts where you could watch the concert on your television, and the stereo broadcast would be on a radio station you could tune to.

I discussed this with Cecelia Hall in the sound department, and Paul Haggar put together a budget for what it would cost. It would add about $100,000 to the film's cost, but I thought it would be worth it. After all, this was the biggest miniseries ever made. The trick was to convince Dan. He could bully it through.

Bernie Gribble thought we were wasting our time, but Gary Smith and I took one of the promo trailers that had been created to publicize *Winds* and set it up to play back in stereo to show Dan what a difference it would make. Because it had been made in stereo, it sounded great. Unfortunately, Dan could not hear stereo, as he was deaf in one ear. To him, it just sounded louder, and the whole demonstration was lost on him. So, we did not make television history by going stereo.

For the next six months Dan and I worked closely on certain sequences. He wanted one of the cutting rooms in Cutting Building One set up as a room he could relax in. He had Paul Haggar, Dawn Steele, and Don Simpson all assembled as he described how he wanted things. They were all afraid of him. I whispered in Dan's ear, "Tell them about the swimming pool on the roof." It was the ear that Dan was deaf in, and my humor went unnoticed.

During this time, Dan did a lot of cutting with me. He would occasionally go down the hall to look at what Burnett and Gary were doing, but most of the time he spent with me. I would arrive every morning at 8:00 to prepare for Dan, who would arrive at 9:00. We would work intensely together until lunch time, and often we had lunch together. Then back to the cutting room until around 6:30 p.m. when Dan's wife would call to make him come home. I would then put the room back together, go home, and drink about half a bottle of scotch to calm down.

Herman Woulk showed up one day on the lot. Dan referred to him affectionately as "the old yid." Woulk described Curtis as "the quickie producer who was going to make it big on Woulk's work." Dan did not want to deal with Woulk, so he asked me to run some scenes for him and take him to lunch.

This was a wonderful opportunity for me. In high school I had read *The Caine Mutiny* in class, and my teacher had said what a great book it was. I told this to Woulk and asked him how he came to write it.

He explained that the articles under which a subordinate can relieve a superior is the breakdown of the chain of command in the military.

"It's never happened at sea in wartime, but it has on the beach," he explained.

Woulk hated the movie version of *The Caine Mutiny* because it only concentrates on the middle section of the novel and ignores the beginning and the end, though he loved Humphrey Bogart's portrayal of Captain Queeg. I feel the movie said everything that the book said despite a Hollywood ending tacked on. Woulk loved *Winds of War* because every word he ever wrote is in it.

Sometimes Dan would outline what he wanted and let me cut ahead. At other times, he did not want me to make a cut unless he was in the room. Mostly we worked on the big "set pieces." This went on for six months.

By the end of that time, Dan and I were often screaming at each other. Finally, Dan said to me, "I can't work with you anymore. I'm going to have to fire you." I told Dan, "You can't do it here. You have to do it on New York Street." We walked over to the New York Street set, and Dan began to explain why he was firing me.

"I know how much this film means to you," he said. "But I can't work with you any longer. You're very talented. I think you should be directing."

Dan started to cry. I put my arm around him and assured him that he was doing the right thing. When we finished, I went to Paul Haggar and told him that I had every reason to expect to be working another six months, and he had better find me a show.

Paul didn't find me a show and I was replaced by Peter Zinner, ACE, so I went to the union. They hired me an expensive lawyer, and I spoke to him for three hours nonstop about what had happened. We sued Paramount. I was the editor of record and should have stayed on until the mix. Of course, they had pulled that cute little trick by putting Bernie in charge.

It was an interesting situation in that Dan would never say I was a bad editor. In fact, he would probably testify for me if he ever showed up to any legal proceeding. However, it was Dan's policy to not show up for legal proceedings. In the end, Paramount offered me about $7,000. My lawyer sweetened the deal by getting the studio to pay my health and welfare for another year. I took the deal.

Judee Gustafson contacted me and said that Dan was messing with my screen credit. I met her on the lot, and she showed me a sample of the credits. I sent word to Dan that he had better not fuck with me since I knew where all the bodies were buried. Dan sent me back a list of how the credits would be. On all of the seven shows, Bernie Gribble would receive top credit as Dan's editor. I would be second on the first two shows and then move down one on each of the other shows. I found it particularly amusing that all names were on the first show, but I was the only person to ever cut on that show.

The Winds of War took its place in television history, and I moved on. It was fourteen months before I got another job. The word was out on me, and I was unhireable. I only got another job by taking a low-paying independent to help a friend. When you have a job, you're hireable. It led to a documentary for HBO and eventually to MGM, where I went back to work for Eric Bercovici.

I talked to Bernie Gribble, ACE about putting *Winds* up for an Emmy. I said we should put up Show Two because it was the most dramatic. The other editors wanted to put up Show Seven because everyone had a credit on it. I knew it was a mistake, but I went along with the group. We were nominated for Show Seven, and we lost to *The Thorn Birds* for the episode where the preacher sleeps with the girl. It was more dramatic, and that's what wins even in an editing competition.

Chapter 13 *Speed*

*I*t is important to be accurate and true in your cutting, but speed is important too. For a time, I worked for Columbia College–Chicago in its Semester in LA project. A number of directing students would come out from Chicago and spend a few weeks working with professionals and directing scenes. Every day, a student would have four hours to direct a scene after having cast it with professionals. He would finish shooting by 6:00 p.m., and at 7:30, he would look at the Editor's Cut and have until 10:00 p.m. to do his own cut.

This happened daily, so the editor had to be fast and accurate because there was no time to slop over into a second day. I was the editor, and I was able to do this every day. My best time was having a cut ready 30 minutes after they turned off the camera. How did I do this?

They shot on DV cam tapes that were loaded into the Avid and edited there. I had an assistant at the set watching the shooting for me. She would text me on the preferred take on every setup. Whenever they changed setups, I would have them break off and rush me the tape to load. I would then get the selected take and start my cut with it.

Now, if the first cut was a master, I would just drop the slate and start after action and then cut the take at cut. When I received a second angle, I would integrate the appropriate pieces into my cut. I would continue this as each new angle arrived. In that manner, I could keep up to camera with the set. When the last shot was made, all I had to do was cut it in and do a polish pass. The secret was to not wait for anything, but make what decisions I could with what I had.

I employ this same technique when I'm working on a feature. I did the first cut on *Shannon's Rainbow* at location during production. By the time they wrapped, I had 92 minutes of cut footage. It was only a first cut, but it was very helpful in determining what was needed. Patrea Patrick took that cut and shaped and finessed it into the final form when she took over for me.

We were shooting on film, and each day new dailies came in. I cut the dailies every day into sequences and did not go home until every possible piece that could be cut was cut. I did not wait for full scenes. If it was a partial, I cut what I had. In that way, I was able to keep current with the set.

I feel it's important to work this way. If you wait around for complete scenes, you'll be buried. When you are buried, it becomes very difficult to dig your way out—particularly when you have to meet a schedule. It's easy to keep adding to scenes as new material comes in. Even if you have only one shot for a scene, you can decide on what parts you will use.

Editing is about constantly making creative decisions as you shape the story. When you decide to make a cut—whether it is good or bad—you are moving forward. After making that cut, you now have an opinion of the cut. If you don't like it, you change it. That moves you forward.

When I'm at a loss for inspiration, I simply start cutting. The mere act of making the cuts will eventually free your creativity, and you will be on the right track.

Chapter 14

Viet Nam: Suppose They Gave a War and Asked Us to Film It

*I*n October of 1966, I landed at Tan Son Nhut airport in Saigon, Viet Nam. It was nearly midnight, but as I emerged from the plane I could hear nearby mortar fire. It was a war, and I was really in it. I was excited, too young and stupid to be scared. I shouldered my B-4 bag and headed for the terminal where I would be picked up. Uncle Sam wanted us to film this historic conflict for posterity.

In 1954, one of the most decisive battles of the twentieth century was fought deep in the interior of Indochina, and most Americans were unaware it was even going on. On May 7, Dien Bien Phu fell to the forces of Ho Chi Minh and his brilliant strategist, General Vo Nguyen Giap. This directly led to the French decision to pull out of their colony in Southeast Asia. American influence forced the partitioning of that country into North and South Vietnam. Free elections eighteen months later were supposed to reunite the country. Since Ho Chi Minh would have undoubtedly won such an election, American influence kept it from happening. After all, Ho was a communist and it was the fifties. I was ten years old and totally unaware that these events would seal my fate and that of so many of my generation.

I dropped out of college in 1963 having not completed my freshman year. I was tired of studying, so I got a job in the shipping room of a department store. It was good to be working and not worrying about tests. After about six months, I received a letter to report for a preinduction physical for the military. In those days, we had a draft and most eligible young men over the age of eighteen were obligated for military service. I thought about my choices: Army, Navy, Marines, Air Force. The Army was too much walking. I couldn't swim, so the Navy was out. The Marines are killers. That left the Air Force, a gentleman's service.

I joined the Air Force. Originally, I was in Intelligence but eventually I was reassigned to film and editing. I was stationed at Vandenberg Air Force Base in Central California. There wasn't much editing to do there. Mostly we watched missile footage and critiqued the footage shot by documentary crews, but I did get a basic grounding in film. The Vietnam War was heating up and I was temporarily assigned to Lookout Mountain Air Force Station in Hollywood.

Lookout was a wonderment to me because it was an actual production facility—a real movie studio. It had a sound stage, a mixing studio, a lab, and many cutting rooms. While there, I was taught many things by the aging editors employed there. Eventually they even let me cut some clips. I learned from the editors that I did not need to be limited by the shots on hand. If an editor needed a shot of a pilot or a plane, it could be taken from previous clips. We told stories, doing whatever was necessary to make them play.

My temporary assignment ended and I was suddenly back at Vandenberg, loaded with excitement and skill and nothing to do. I volunteered for duty in Vietnam. It wasn't that I was patriotic. I wanted to get out of Vandenberg Air Force Base and into a production unit like Lookout Mountain Air Force Station. The only way out of Vandenberg was to volunteer for Vietnam, and so I did. I figured after a year there I could transfer back to Lookout.

I lucked out in my flight overseas. At Travis Air Force Base, it was announced that tickets were available for Pan Am Flight One Round the World. The tickets were for some officers, but they didn't have passports so they had to fly military. I had a passport, so I flew to Bangkok via Honolulu, Tokyo, and Hong Kong in style instead of in the back of a C-141.

I was assigned to Khorat Royal Thai Air Force Base, but film equipment had not yet arrived. Having not been given any indication as to what the Air Force's overall plan was, I didn't know what to do. Basically, the men there were mounting cameras on planes and then downloading them. I started ordering editing equipment, and in doing so I was sending a coded message to command at Tan Son Nhut that there was an editor at Khorat. I quickly received a call from the 600th Photo Squadron telling me to get down to Saigon in double time.

I received orders and suddenly I was on a plane to Tan Son Nhut in the Republic of Viet Nam. I arrived in the middle of the night, greeted by the sound of mortar shells exploding. I was to learn this was a constant sound. I was picked up by Airmen Hartung, Gist, and Roberge and taken to midnight chow. Afterwards, I was assigned a bunk to sleep in.

The next morning, I was taken over to editorial, which was located in a trailer where Staff Sgt. Tom Young was in charge. He showed me the drill. The Air Force planes had cameras mounted on them. They had forward and aft blister cameras, forward and aft pod cameras, and gun cameras. After a mission, the cameras would be downloaded and brought to the lab in the 600th Photo Squadron here at Tan Son Nhut. After developing, the footage came to the editors who viewed and decided its value. If there was nothing on it, the film was returned to the pilot. If there were good bomb hits or gun hits, we would order a designated number of prints and the original would be forwarded to Lookout Mountain. The footage really had no military significance. It was used for briefings; essentially, we were making stock footage for future films.

Sgt. Young assigned me a shift, and I began working. Before that I was offered a cup of Beam coffee, which everyone started the day with. It was coffee with a shot of Jim Beam bourbon in it. You started the day with a buzz.

The footage was shot on 16 mm reversal film similar to what home movies were on. The stock was Kodak MS 7256. First it was developed as a negative and then it was redeveloped as a positive image. Then it would come to us to view on a Moviola Library Reader, which was gentle on the film, and we would decide if it needed to go for printing. If so, we attached leaders and named it.

Figure 14.1. Author working at a Library Reader.

Besides viewing film, we often had to do a shift of building bunkers. Ours were made from large metal shipping crates like you see on cargo ships. We then surrounded the structure with sandbags we filled ourselves. In an attack, we were designated to run to the nearest bunker for safety. We heard mortar fire constantly, and every now and then one came over the fence. The Viet Cong were fond of walking them in to the target by firing and readjusting and firing again.

I met Airman Howard, who was the squadron film librarian. He made it clear that he wanted no part of Vietnam or the war. He arrived at Tan Son Nhut on a contract airline. Many men came over that way. The Air Force contracted with several of the big airlines to fly GIs to Vietnam. When they returned, they brought back coffins with our soldiers in them.

Airman Howard emerged into the Southeast Asian sun and stood at the top of the stairs surveying the airport. He looked at the pretty stewardess standing by him and announced for all the world, and hopefully President Johnson, to hear, "I hate this fucking place!" He startled the stewardess and then picked up his duffel bag and descended into the war.

During his time in country, he would walk around making obscene gestures and explaining to everyone, "I hate this fucking place." Officers or enlisted men, it didn't matter. He treated everyone the same. He was never disciplined for this. After all, what could they do: send him to Vietnam? I think he was trying to get a medical discharge for being crazy. Where we were, it didn't matter. Crazy was the norm.

Life became a routine for me. I would pull my shift and then go into Saigon to drink and fraternize. This routine was broken a few times. Once I accompanied some men as a gunner when they went to visit an orphanage that we sponsored. We drove there in an Air Force station wagon. I was crouched in the back with an M-16. One of the NCOs I was with said, "I hope that kid knows how to handle that weapon." I did. I had taken the training at Vandenberg. I was a terrible shot, so the instructor told me, "Look kid, just put it on automatic and spray them. You'll be fine." Fortunately, I didn't kill anyone. Nothing of note happened other than I got to handle an M-16 and see some of the countryside.

Another time, I was sitting in the barracks when I noticed there was no sound of mortar fire. I was about to mention this when a huge explosion occurred. The Viet Cong had blown up the ammo dump at Long Binh.

One night the Cong fired a number of mortar rounds over the fence at us. Everyone ran to the bunker except me, who slept through it. After it was over, one of the men woke me to tell me what happened.

"Is it over?" I asked.

"Yes," he replied.

"Then why did you wake me?"

As I was starting my second month at Tan Son Nhut, we received word that the detachment at Khorat was being made into the 601st Photo Flight and would be receiving a photo lab with an editing subsystem like the one we had. I was ordered to fly there and take over the editing department.

I and the system arrived back in Thailand, and we set it up. Houston Fearless corporation provide us with three trailers, which were off-loaded from two C-141s. We positioned them on concrete pads and began setting up. The trailers expanded by cranking them out to double trailers. One was the lab complete with an ME4 processor and a printer. One was an office, and the last one was the editing subsystem. It consisted of two editing rooms with equipment, a projection room, and a booth for both project-ing and recording narration.

MSgt. Humphries was in charge of the lab, and I ran editorial under him. Very quickly we were up and running, and all the film from Thailand came to us instead of Tan Son Nhut. From Thailand, the Air Force was bombing North Vietnam. I was assigned a few airmen who were cross-training from still photo into motion picture. I was to train them in the routine I had learned at Tan Son Nhut. We ran two twelve-hour shifts.

Looking at the footage on the Library Reader, I began to see little white things every now and then. They were only on maybe two frames. I asked one of the pilots what they were, and he replied, "SAMs." SAMs are surface-to-air missiles. Since most of our footage was coming from planes flying over the North, we realized that the people on the ground were shooting everything they could at the planes. Sometimes the planes were shot down, and the pilots became residents of the Hanoi Hilton.

One of the pilots would come in when I wasn't there and use the equipment to edit his film together. I was very territorial and put up a sign saying only editorial personnel could use the equipment. At some point, I realized this was a mistake. The pilots had to fly one hundred missions over the North before they went home. Many would not make it. The worse that was likely to happen to me was to pick up some exotic venereal disease.

I decided that whatever the pilots wanted, I would supply. I would edit their footage. If there was a movie they liked playing at the 16 mm theatre on base, I would copy it for them. I'd learned to print; I would have MSgt. Humphries put a printing light on it, and I would make the print. It wouldn't have sound, but the picture would be there.

On their part, the pilots would bring me Heineken beer and Suntory whiskey from Japan. One day a pilot came to me because President Johnson was limiting the targets that could be bombed. He knew someone on the ground was shooting at him, and he wanted to get them. He brought in some film from his aircraft, and I ran it while he studied a map to figure out where the enemy was.

We spotted little flashes of light coming from the ground. It was antiaircraft fire. The pilot carefully examined his map and was able to figure out where the groundfire was coming from. He smiled. "Gotcha! Next trip a bomb's gonna fall off my plane on those people," he told me.

Many things were going on at Khorat. One night, Brigadier General Jimmy Stewart of the Air Force Reserves came through. I totally missed him. Bob Hope brought his USO Christmas Show to the base. I missed that too.

Besides the footage coming in from the planes, we had a few documentary crews in the field. They would shoot stories of human interest to be sent back to the states for television to use as filler on their news shows. One of them tried flying backseat in a F-105 on a bombing run over the North. After releasing its bombs, the plane went into a series of maneuvers to avoid being hit by SAMs and antiaircraft fire. They were quite violent, and the cameraman threw up all over the backseat. Back on the ground, the pilot told the cameraman he'd kill him if he ever came near his plane again.

I was approached by a sergeant from the documentary crews. He told me that a general was coming in a few days to inspect the base. He wanted to make a film of it

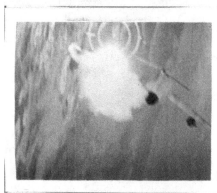

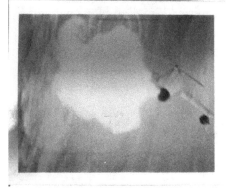

Figure 14.2. MiG kill.

for the general. We got together with MSgt. Humphries and came up with a plan. When the general landed, a camera crew filmed him. This film was immediately rushed to the lab, and Humphries men developed it. He brought it to me, and I cut together what I had.

As the general toured various places, camera crews would rush the film to the lab. I would cut it together and expand the clip. By the time the general reached the 601st Photo Flight, I had cut his whole tour of the base. As he walked in we ran the cut on the big screen. He was thrilled, and we gave the film to him. It was good PR for photo since we were considered a nonessential part of the war.

We in the support people of the war effort were considered REMPs. Roughly translated, that stands for Rear Echelon Motherfuckers. We were support, but many support people were killed in the war. I know of at least two cameramen who were killed while I was there. No one was untouched by the Vietnam War.

Captain Chris Nyby II came up from Vietnam and was assigned to the 601st. He was the son of Christian Nyby who had won the Academy Award for his editing of *Red River* and had gone on to direct the original version of *The Thing*. I was constantly asking him questions about Hollywood and the business.

One evening we received gun camera footage of a couple of MiG kills. One was so spectacular that it ended up in *Life* magazine after we sent it on to Lookout. This and other footage we would build into a Commander's Briefing Clip that we had to have ready every day by 5:00 p.m. Capt. Nyby would take the clip and go to the briefing. One time I asked about the military significance of the clip reel. He said, "There is none. It's something they run after the briefing while they're drinking."

That bothered me to some extent because of the work and effort that went into the clip. Mostly what we were doing was collecting historical footage to end up in future films. They have been doing this in all wars since World War I. The only difference was better quality film and shooting in color.

We did make a briefing film for incoming troops on the dos and don'ts of living in Thailand. It was a full production that we shot around the area, and I edited it together. It was silent so when shown, someone had to narrate. The main thing I learned working in Southeast Asia was how to tell a story by using shots from other clips to make the story work.

As 1966 rolled into 1967, I was called back to Saigon to help out. I spent another month there and almost won the war for the Viet Cong. Because all of our film was classified, we had to dispose of it by burning it. This meant unwinding rolls of film and then jamming them into paper bags. One morning I was sent with another man out near the flight line to burn film in metal barrels. We were both suffering from hangovers after a particularly hard night of drinking in town.

We loaded as many bags as possible into the barrels and ignited them. Some of the film fell out of the barrel into the tall grass and ignited it. In my confused state, I watched this with disinterest. Suddenly, I remembered watching a forest fire come over a hill outside Santa Barbara the year before. It moved very fast, and there was little chance of stopping it.

I screamed at my companion and immediately started throwing dirt on the fire. He saw what was happening and joined me in trying to smother the flames. It was touch and go for a time, but eventually we were able to smother it all. It was the dry season, and if we had not stopped it when we did the whole of Tan Son Nhut Air Base might have burned. Destroying the base was something the Viet Cong were unable to do.

After about a month, I rotated back to Khorat in Thailand. Everything was going like a well-oiled routine there. I never believed while I was in Southeast Asia that I would ever go home. My day to day activities were the world to me. America was a distant memory. I could not imagine that my DEROS (Date Estimated Return Over Seas) would ever happen. It did in August.

I was ordered to Bangkok to catch a flight home. Instead of catching the Air Force flight, I decided to go by train through the jungle to the city. A friend came with me. It was exciting to travel with the Thai people on their train. Every time we stopped, vendors would come up to our windows with exotic foods to buy.

At one point we stopped in the middle of the jungle; I got out and took pictures. Then it was on to Bangkok and a plane ride to the "Land of the Big BX." I saw sunrise twice on the long trip to

Figure 14.3. The train stopped in the jungle.

California. I did not have a chance to shave or bathe, so I had to avoid the Air Police when I arrived back in California.

Coming back, I was offered the choice of being assigned to the East Coast or the West Coast. I picked the West Coast, figuring I'd be assigned to Lookout Air Force Station in Hollywood. It was all for naught. They sent me to Vandenberg, right back where I started from.

Chapter 15

Television Changes Everything

W hen television came along in the late 1940s, it changed everything. Suddenly, there was a device in the house that gave you moving pictures with sound. On news shows you could see as well as hear what was being reported. Originally, there were variety shows and live television dramas. To fill up the air time, old movies were needed, too, but there was a problem.

Television is an electronic medium. First invented in the late 1920s, and later demonstrated at the 1939 World's Fair in New York, it became commercially available in the late 1940s. Because of the electronics, television was broadcast at 30 frames per second (fps). Each frame was made up of two fields: an odd field and an even field. This meant 60 fields per second, which put it in phase with power, which was 60 cycles per second. This became NTSC, and in Europe, where the power was 50 cycles, television went to 25 frames per second, the PAL system.

Now movies run at 24fps, and TV runs at 30 fps. This creates a problem in running a movie on television. It won't work. However, a way to make it work was devised. It was called the 3:2 pull-down system. It's based on making four frames into five frames without adding a new frame. How is this possible?

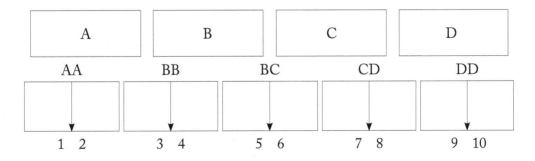

This is how it works: the A frame pulls down to fields 1 and 2. The B frame pulls down to fields 3 and 4. Now, here is where the trick comes in. One of the B fields repeats itself in field 5. Then the C frame pulls down into fields 6 and 7. The D frame pulls down into fields 8 and 9. Then, like the B frame, the D repeats a field, into field 10. Six times four is twenty-four, but six times five becomes thirty.

In this manner, it was possible to project 24fps films at 30fps to the television audience. It was a major breakthrough, because now television shows could be filmed like movies and shown on TV. We were no longer limited to shooting on sets and broadcasting live. A whole show could be shot on film, edited, and presented over the airways. This created a whole new industry of television.

The first great empire of television was Desilu. Desi Arnaz, a band leader and some-time actor, and his wife, Lucille Ball, an MGM starlet, got together to create *I Love Lucy*, the first monster hit of television. CBS wanted Lucy to reprise her role in the radio series *My Favorite Husband*. She wanted to do a series with her husband. CBS did not want Desi, but Lucy stuck to her guns, and a pilot was made and shows were ordered.

Figure 15.1. Danny Cahn, ACE with Jack Tucker, ACE at the 2000 Eddies, where both won awards.

Into this situation came a young editor named Danny Cahn, ACE. He was second generation, the son of Phil Cahn, who worked at Universal. William Asher had been offered the job, but he was more interested in developing as a director, so he referred the job to Danny. Jess Oppenheimer, the producer/production manager, hired him.

Desi Arnaz told CBS that he wanted the series shot on film. Desi, Lucy, Danny, and cinematographer Karl Freund (who had directed the original *The Mummy*) had all come from film. The writers, Bob Carroll, Jr., and Madelyn Davis, were from radio. CBS balked at the idea of shooting film. They told Desi that if he wanted it on film, he could pay for it. Desi replied, "I will, but I will own the negatives." That was the first of many smart decisions he made.

Those shows are still playing today around the world. You can buy them on DVD and Blu-ray. Money is still being generated because of the quality of the comedy and the fact that the show was shot on film. Many a videotaped show was erased and no longer exists, but film lasts.

It was decided that *I Love Lucy* would be filmed before a live audience as a four-camera show. This presented several problems, one of which was how to light for four cameras. Karl Freund developed flat lighting, which is still used today for sitcoms. A

Figure 15.2. The Monster Moviola for running three cameras.

large slate and clapper was built so that all four cameras could sync to it. The editing process was revolutionary.

Desi and Danny had Moviola build a special machine that became known as "the Monster." It had four picture heads and one sound head. The assistant, Bud Molin, had to sync four work prints to one sound track. It would be built in ten-minute reels and then mounted on the Monster. Editor Danny Cahn would then go through and mark which picture was to be used where. There would be a wide shot and various close-ups and medium shots. Danny would mark the picture, and then Bud could assemble it into a single strand.

Then the show could be finished on a regular Moviola, where it was adjusted for pacing. The Monster was needed only for the first pass. It became the standard on all multicamera sitcoms. It was still being used when I came to Paramount in 1980 on *Happy Days* and *Mork & Mindy*. I eventually bought the Monster and kept it for a time before selling it to the Lucy Museum in upstate New York.

Because of the success of *Lucy*, the production company went on to film *The Danny Thomas Show*, with its spinoff, *The Andy Griffith Show*, and several others made under the banner of Desilu. Desi proved to be a brilliant business man and Lucy an extraordinary comedian. They flourished, and Danny Cahn became head of their post-production. He gave many prominent editors their start. One was a young man named Michael Kahn, ACE, who went on to become Steven Spielberg's editor.

Quinn Martin was a sound editor at Universal who was cutting in the dialogue for Francis, the Talking Mule, when Danny grabbed him. He came to Desilu to cut sound effects on *I Love Lucy* and wound up as the producer of the original *The Untouchables*. Later, he formed QM Productions, which created the series *The Fugitive* and *The Invaders*.

Eventually, Desi and Lucy split up. She bought him out of the studio, and Desilu continued on until the end of the 1960s. The company produced the original *Star Trek* series. Desi left, and Danny went off to pursue a career in directing with Lee Marvin on the *M Squad* series. The effects of television on film editing and the business as a whole were revolutionary.

Because in the 1950s television sets were small—twenty-eight inches was the size of the largest screen—editing had to be rethought. In the 1940s many scenes played out in master shots. They were playing on a large screen, and the audience could see the details. On television, close-ups became very important in telling the story. This began to filter into theatrical films. Close-ups were used more often.

Also, TV shows began developing a hook to lure viewers into the show. Instead of starting with the main title, a show would open with something exciting in progress to get your attention and keep you from switching channels. Movies began to use this device, too. Traditionally, there would be a main title and credits, and then the story would begin. Now the film might run ten minutes before getting to the title.

In addition, end credits, which were developed in television, began to spill over into features. Whatever was happening on the tube would eventually make it to the big screen. Initially, the studios were at war with television. All manner of things was created to lure people back into the theaters and out of their living rooms. 3D, a device first developed in silent films, was brought back, dusted off, and put before the cameras. It lasted about a year before fading away. In 1952 the first Cinerama film was released. It was basically a travelogue but in an exciting new film process.

Developed from an Air Force gunnery training tool, the Cinerama technique involved a camera with three lenses, exposing three separate negatives. When printed, it was played back on three separate projectors on a curved screen, which created an illusion of depth because of peripheral vision. This was definitely not something you could see on television. Playing in only one theater in New York for three months, that first Cinerama picture became the highest-grossing film of 1952.

This Is Cinerama, the original film, opened modestly in black and white, with a standard 1:33 to 1 image. Lowell Thomas, newsman and adventurer, talked about the advances in filmmaking, ending with his declaring, "This is Cinerama." The curtains

Figure 15.3. Cinerama set up.

Figure 15.4. The butt splicer for editing magnetic track.

on the screen opened wider and wider to reveal an image six times larger on a curved screen. The audience watched as they ascended a roller coaster to the top. Then it started its descent as the audience screamed.

It was one of the most exciting moments in film history. The effect was incredible. You could feel it in the pit of your stomach. You were in the movie. The use of seven-track stereophonic sound enhanced the process.

Cinerama was a bitch to edit, however. There was no Moviola for this. The film actually ran at 26fps instead of 24fps, and each frame was 6 perfs long, as opposed to the normal 35 mm 4 perf. Shots were assembled over the bench through a synchronizer, and you had to project them to see how they worked. It was just like the silent days before the Moviola.

Because of the tremendous torque on the projectors, splices had to be reinforced with Mylar tape to keep them from opening. This introduced the butt splicer into the editing room. Traditionally, shots were cut and stuck together with paper clips. Then the reel went to the assistant to weld together on a pedestal hot splicer with glue. With the butt splicer, the editor could make his own splice with tape and immediately run the cut on the Moviola. At this point, the industry had stopped using optical soundtracks for editing. By 1950 magnetic tracks were taking over, and the butt splicer was perfect for this.

Cinerama hung around for about ten years. It could be seen only in special theaters in big cities. Several travelogues were made, and in the early 1960s, MGM made two features using the process. One was George Pal's *The Wonderful World of the Brothers Grimm*, and the other was *How the West Was Won*. *West* became the last film to be made using this process. Playing only in Cinerama theaters, it became the highest-grossing film of 1962 and won an Oscar for its editor, Harold Kress, ACE.

By the time Stanley Kramer was ready to make a third Cinerama feature, *It's a Mad, Mad, Mad, Mad World*, it was decided that the process was too difficult, and he shot that film in Super Panavision 70, but retained the name Cinerama. In Hollywood the Cinerama Dome was built for that feature, but it never actually ran a Cinerama film until the early twenty-first century.

The process that really held for movies was CinemaScope. It was an anamorphic process wherein a wide lens would capture an image in the ratio of 2:35 to 1 and compress it into a normal 1:33 to 1 frame. Played back with a compensating lens, it would be 2:35 to 1 on a theater screen. No glasses were needed, and, unlike with Cinerama, only one projector was needed.

By the mid-1950s, the studios realized that they should get into the television business. Disney and Warner Bros. were first, but MGM and Universal were not far behind. They also realized that they could promote their features with their television shows. *Warner Bros. Presents* and *MGM Parade* would devote part of their shows to behind-the-scenes previews of upcoming features.

Television was also a training ground for future stars, directors, cinematographers, and editors. They could start on the small screen and transition to the big one. Some were able to do this, while some were not.

Originally, in the early 1950s, dramatic TV shows were shot live in New York. The time zones in the United States created a problem with this. When a show came on in the Big Apple at 7:00 p.m., it was 4:00 p.m. on the West Coast. How could a show be broadcast on the West Coast at 7:00?

The solution was Kinescope. This was a process wherein a show could be filmed off a monitor. It would be 7:00 in New York, and the live show would be fed to the West Coast, where it would be filmed off the monitor. Because it was 4:00 in LA, the editor had two hours in which to develop the film, sync it to its soundtrack, and have it ready for broadcast at 7:00 p.m. West Coast time. Kinescope is the only reason that some of these old live shows have survived. Kinescope was replaced in 1956 with the invention of videotape.

Now shows could be videotaped live and played back on the West Coast. It also meant that shows could be recorded early and actually edited. The first editing was done with a razor blade and tape and was not a precise thing. Eventually, it was decided that the best way to edit was from tape recorder to tape recorder.

It was also decided that films could be transferred to tape using the 3:2 pull-down and then be available for direct broadcast. This is a process called "telecine," wherein film is converted to a tape image. During the process, time code is generated on the tape itself. Like key numbers on film, the time code identifies each frame. You could even edit a film on tape, but it was a slow, linear process. If you wanted to change a cut by lengthening it, you had to go back and relay all the shots again, because when going from tape to tape, there was a loss in quality. You didn't want to be more than a generation away.

In the 1960s, when color television came out, a problem occurred. When color was broadcast at 30fps, there was a hum. It was discovered that this hum went away if you slowed down slightly, to 29.97fps. This was fine, but what did it do to 3:2 pull-down? It was discovered that if you slowed down from 24fps in telecine to 23.98fps, the 3:2 worked the same as 24 to 30.

But there was another problem. Where do we put the color information on the tape? With black and white, the time code and real time matched perfectly. Sixty minutes of time code ran exactly sixty minutes. When the color information was added between frames, it threw everything off. Now sixty minutes of time code actually ran longer than sixty minutes. It was sixty minutes plus 3.59 seconds.

To deal with this, a new time code was created. It was called "drop frame." In this system, every minute frames 0 and 1 are dropped, except on the tenth minute. So, at the end of sixty minutes, the code reads sixty minutes also. So, for example, at 01;08;59;29, the next code reads 01;09;00;02. (Drop frame is displayed in semi-colons.)

The code that counts every frame was called "non-drop frame." It is displayed in colons. The tape is the same; it merely differs in which time code you are using. Drop frame is time accurate. Non-drop frame is frame accurate. On a film-based show, you would want non-drop frame, because every frame of film is important.

Credits

Fig. 15.3: Copyright © 1954 by Cinerama Films, Inc.

Chapter 16 *Color*

From the early days of cinema, filmmakers wanted to put color into their films. It was common to tint prints in various colors. I once had a 16 mm print of the original *Phantom of the Opera*. Night scenes and scenes beneath the opera house were tinted blue. The ball scene with the Red Death was tinted red. This was common during the silent era and even later. In 1950 the black and white film *Rocketship X-M* had the scenes on Mars tinted red.

The Technicolor Motion Picture Corporation was founded by Herbert Kalmus, Daniel Frost Comstock, and W. Burton Wescott in 1914. The name was based on the fact that both Kalmus and Comstock had received their undergraduate degrees from the Massachusetts Institute of Technology. They originally came up with a color process by which images were exposed onto two separate black and white negatives in the same camera. Split by a prism, one negative was through a green filter and the other through a red filter. Then a print had to be made using a dye transfer process with the information from both negatives.

This was replaced by the three-strip process (yellow, cyan, magenta) which became the standard for Hollywood color films of the thirties and forties. It required a great deal of light to properly expose for this process. It also meant that for everything shot, there were three black and white negatives exposed through color filters, which made color films very expensive.

By 1950 a process was invented that allowed color to be shot on a single roll of negative. The film consisted of three layers of emulsion: red, green, and blue. This made color photography more affordable. However, since this emulsion was composed of vegetable dyes, the color could fade over time. To preserve the color, it was necessary to make a YCM on three black and white stocks, which does not fade because it is silver halides.

Timing, which on film is color correction, was done with colored discs that could be put over the shot to indicate how much of a color to use in the printing. Eventually, the Hazeltine machine was invented. The timer could run the negative through the machine, producing a positive image. There were three knobs, representing red, green, and blue, that could be adjusted, and the timer could judge what printing lights to use for each color.

A first trial answer print would be struck, and the timer and the producer or director would view it. The timer would take notes from that screening and further adjustments would be made. The process would be repeated until a perfect print was struck. Once that was done, an interpositive was printed with the same lights. From that, an internegative was made and then, after a check print, release printing could begin.

In the 1990s, digital intermediates began to emerge. Initially in the digital age, certain shots were captured as a file in a computer, and they would be enhanced or a CGI (computer generated image) would be added. After color correction the image would then go back to film for cutting into the movie. What if this could be done to a whole film?

The cost of going in and out was prohibitive. It was four dollars a frame to go into the computer and another four to come out. At twenty-four frames per second that meant it cost about one hundred dollars a second to go in and to come out. Eventually these costs came down and capturing a whole feature was possible. The digital intermediate, or DI, was born.

There are great advantages to color correcting in a computer. You can change a portion of a frame instead of the whole frame. A power window can be drawn around a portion of the frame and all changes would be within the window. You can change seasons by changing the color of the leaves on the trees. There is no need to make a print until everything looks just right.

As always with technological innovations, the downside is to make us more forgiving on the set.

"Don't worry about how it looks. We'll fix it in the DI."

From the color-corrected DI a negative can then be made for release printings. Today it is more likely a DCP (digital cinema package) would be made since so many theaters are digital. The DI can become a universal master from which anything that is needed can be created.

The AVID has color correction as part of its software, as does FCP and Premiere. Some editors I know use this to achieve a look to their cuts. I never do this. I want someone with twenty to thirty years of experience doing my color correction. Nowadays, most post houses are using DaVinci Resolve to handle this. The software is available for anyone who wants to download it.

I prefer to be a film editor. I am an expert in telling stories with pictures and sound. That is enough for me. If I need color correction or special effects done to my story, I want to go to someone who specializes in it. The editing systems are set up to make us auteurs, Jacks-of-all-trades, and masters of none. I want to be a master of editing.

Filmmaking has always been a collaborative medium. I think that is a good part of the magic. I have heard of some people who do everything on their film: write, direct, star, shoot, edit, compose the music, and mix the film. They should also be compelled to watch their film. The bringing together of many artists led by a creative artist, usually the director, is what makes for great movies. The real magic is in the collaboration of talented artists.

Chapter 17 *Reels*

Figure 17.1. Reels of film in shipping case. Photo courtesy of Victoria Hamilton.

I n our brave new world of the twenty-first century, editing has become much less a physical activity and more of an exercise in the Ethernet. Where we once actually cut film and spliced it together to tell a story, we now deal with files for the same objective. The physicality of what we did was both limiting and liberating.

The standard format for professional film is 35 mm. It runs at 24 frames per second, and 90 feet of film runs one minute at that rate. Nine hundred feet is ten minutes,

Figure 17.2. 1,000-foot reel. Photo courtesy of Victoria Hamilton.

which fits on a 1,000-foot Goldberg reel nicely. At that size, it is reasonably easy to work with the material. Early films of the silent era were often one-reelers.

Besides the standard Goldberg reels, split reels were developed to deal with film coming directly from the lab. Film from the lab is delivered on cores. With a split reel, the film can be directly dealt with instead of having to rewind it onto a Goldberg reel.

As stories developed beyond the one-reel concept, we simply added reels. To accommodate this, projection booths were equipped with two projectors. Reel 1 would mount on projector 1 and run. As it finished, the projectionist would switch to projector 2, which contained reel 2. To make

Figure 17.3. Split Reel. Photo courtesy of Victoria Hamilton.

the changeover from reel 1 to reel 2 seamless and undetectable, cue marks were placed at the end of reel 1. These were little circles in the upper right-hand corner of the frame and looked like cigarette burns. The first one was 12 feet before the end of the picture and the second one 24 frames before the end.

When the first cue appeared, the projectionist would start the second projector. Each reel had an Academy countdown leader that was 12 feet from the picture start in the leader to the actual first frame of the picture. When the projectionist saw the second cue, he had one second to switch from projector 1 to projector 2. An experienced projectionist could do this without the audience realizing what was happening. Because of this, a movie could have as many reels as necessary to tell its story.

Print stock came in 2,000-foot rolls. To expedite printing, ten-minute reels (900 feet) were combined into 20-minute reels (1,800 feet). Reels 1 and 2 became big reel 1; reels 3 and 4 became big reel 2; reels 5 and 6 became big reel 3; and so on. Because of the fact that on a release print the sound is 20 frames ahead of the picture, this did create a problem in combining reels. It was solved by adding a 20-frame pullup of the beginning of reel 2 on the end of reel 1. The first 20 frames of sound of reel 2 were reprinted and added to the end of reel 1. Therefore, when the sound was pulled up and the reels were combined, the frames lost in cutting the first frame picture of reel 2 were replaced by the last 20 frames of reel 1. This made the combining flawless.

Figure 17.4. 2,000-foot Projection Reel. Photo courtesy of Victoria Hamilton.

Because mistakes could happen in changeover, it was important to break reels in just the right spot. It couldn't happen on a critical cut. It was best to end a reel at the end of a scene. Also, there should be no dialogue or music in the last second of the old reel or the first second of the new reel. Music should not cross reels. For example, in Robert Wise's *The Sound of Music*, at the end of reel 1, Julie Andrews is singing as she approaches the von Trapp home. She stops to look at the house in wonder, and the music stops. The reel changes, and she and the music pick up again.

This is how things were throughout most of the twentieth century. We cut in ten-minute reels and printed in 20-minute reels. With the advent of digital editing, this began to change. Initially, the movie was shot on film and the dailies were printed. In this way, the director and editor, cinematographer, et al. could see their work on the big screen like God and DeMille intended. It made it easy to judge performance.

For editing, the dailies would then be digitized and loaded into the Avid (or whatever system was used). After a cut was accomplished digitally, a cut list would be created, and a film-conforming crew would come in and cut the film dailies to match the digital cut. Then, the cut would be viewed on the big screen on film. When changes were made, the film crew would adjust the print. This way, the movie was evaluated on the big screen and not on a computer.

When hi-def came in, fewer people were making and conforming prints. They were content to make their evaluations on a big monitor. Since we were no longer conforming, it became unnecessary to edit in ten-minute reels. We started simply working in 20-minute reels, which, when complete, would generate a cut list for the negative cutter, who would conform the negative for finalization in the lab.

Now that there is very little print making, the physical need for reels has mostly disappeared. Should we abandon the concept of reels altogether or maintain the reels beyond the physical need? I think we should keep them for several reasons. If you have a number of reels, one person can work on a reel while another can be on a different reel. When I was doing the *Jessie* television series, I would often divide my change notes from the director with my assistant, Ruth Bird. She would take three reels and I would take three; consequently, we could make the changes very quickly.

It also makes the work more manageable. As Maureen O'Connell tells me, in art, it's called limiting your palette. If you deal in sections, it's not so overwhelming. The thought of editing *The Winds of War* as a whole—at 18 hours—is daunting, but taking each of the 108 reels one at a time is quite workable.

My business partner, Patrea Patrick, and I attended a writing workshop. The teacher advised the writers to think and write in reels: in reel 1, this should happen; in reel 2, that should happen; and so on. I asked Mark Helfrich, ACE, about his experience editing *Hercules*. Though I doubt many prints were struck of it, he said that he cut the film in 20-minute reels.

Therefore, my opinion is that there is little physical reason to work in 20-minute reels, but for artistic reasons, it still has validity.

Chapter 18

The Roger Corman School of Filmmaking

A t one of the American Cinema Editors annual Eddie Awards ceremonies, Roger Corman was given the Filmmaker of the Year award. There were some who thought this strange since he was mostly known for low-budget, non-union films shot in a matter of days. We on the board of directors were honoring him for the many filmmakers who got their start working for him. A few of the many are Francis Ford Coppola, Martin Scorsese, Ron Howard, Joe Dante, Jack Nicholson, Mark Goldblatt, Tina Hirsch, John Gilbert, Monte Hellman, and Sylvester Stallone.

All of these people are considered to be graduates of the Roger Corman School of Filmmaking, which I personally believe was the best school to learn the business. The difference between it and USC, UCLA, CSU, NYU, and Chapman is that at Corman it was real. Even though I teach at a university film school, I think students got a better education from Roger. You didn't concern yourself with getting an A; you had to finish on time with a film that made money.

Many of the former students were proud of the training they got and had made jackets that said Roger Corman School of Filmmaking, and I thought ACE should have one made for Roger. I knew he was too cheap to have bought one, so I borrowed John Gilbert's, and we had one made for Roger. Tom Rolf presented it to him at the ceremony.

Roger Corman received a bachelor of science degree in industrial engineering from Stanford University. He worked four days in that profession before quitting and going to work at 20th Century Fox as a reader in the script department to follow something he cared more about. He eventually sold a script for the movie *Highway Dragnet*, which was the beginning of his career. He produced his first film, *Monster from the Ocean Floor*, with money he earned from the script. It was successful and followed by *The Fast and the Furious*.

Corman is most known for his association with American International Pictures, where he did a number of low-budget monster films like *It Conquered the World* and *Not of This Earth*. He eventually created the Edgar Allan Poe Horror Series, beginning with *The Fall of the House of Usher*. With Corman's highly exploitive films and the *Beach Party* series, AIP created the "youth market" that still dominates the film industry today.

I was not fortunate enough to have ever worked for Roger, but I have heard many of the stories. Some of them may have gone like this:

ROGER: Well now, you've been editing here for a couple of weeks. Do you like it?

EMPLOYEE: Yes, very much. Thank you for this opportunity.

ROGER: I've been looking at your work. I think you might be ready to direct.

EMPLOYEE: Direct? Me? I would kill for the chance.

ROGER: Good. Of course, you'll have to take a little cut in pay.

And so on.

Budding directors would have to do a healthy number of setups every day and get by without having permits, but if they could handle it, a career was opening up for them. Roger could make a nickel scream, but it was good discipline for the young filmmakers. Corman is supposed to have said to a young Ron Howard, who was about to helm his first film, *Grand Theft Auto*, "If you do a good job with this, you'll never have to work for me again."

Ron did do a good job, and he often has given Roger small parts in his films, as have many other graduates. John Gilbert edited the remake of *Piranha*. The original version had been done fifteen years earlier with Mark Goldblatt and Joe Dante editing. Roger explained to John, "We won't have to reshoot the fish. They're underwater and the film won't look dated. One fish looks much like another one."

Roger made a tax deal with Ireland to set up a studio and make films there. To avoid paying an import tax on the AVID, Corman had Gilbert carry it as part of his personal baggage. This is when AVIDs weren't software based. There was a lot of hardware that was part of the system that he had to take in his baggage. Roger reimbursed him for the $700 overage fee. He then had to put the system together without tech support. Nevertheless, John Gilbert learned his lessons well and moved on to better projects.

Jack Nicholson worked on many of Corman's films, but among them, *The Little Shop of Horrors* stands out. It was supposedly shot in two days, and Nicholson gives an outstanding performance as a dental patient who loves pain.

As Roger Corman was to filmmaking, Ted Gomillion was to sound. A graduate of the USC Film School, he started out recording location sound. At some point, Gomillion came up with the idea of creating trailers that could be taken on location featuring 35 mm projection so looping, the replacing of dialog, could be done in them immediately instead of having to wait to get back to the studio, perhaps months later. It can be very difficult for an actor to have to revoice a part he finished two pictures back. This was a great advantage for location shooting and was used on the 1970's *Too Late the Hero*.

In the trailer you could also watch dailies in sync with picture, which is sometimes difficult to do on location.

Gomillion was instrumental in creating the ADR system that we use today instead of looping. Instead of having to cut loops that played the line over and over again, Ted computerized it so the system would run down to the line, play it and play it again. He created the three-beeps system for cueing in the actors where they were supposed to replace the dialog. He customized the Simplex projectors to work at high speed. This was long before digital was even imagined.

Sound was built on 35 mm reels and mounted on dummies in the machine room. Dummies are recorders that only play sound and do not record. They were interlocked with the projector as if played back and forth. If Ted thought a track was out of sync, he would stop and call the machine room on the intercom. "Move effects track seven four frames forward." He would wait for what he thought was long enough and yell into the intercom, "Watch your fingers!" as he pushed the go button. The dummy loaders were quick to move their hands.

Ted took over a building in Hollywood; founded Gomillion Studios; and built a mixing stage, an ADR room, a foley stage, and everything else a modern sound studio needed. The staff included many future stars of the sound editing world: Richard Anderson (*Raiders of the Lost Ark*); Stephen Hunter Flick (*Speed*); Teresa Eckton (*Never Cry Wolf*); Bob Deschaine, the ADR mixer; and Bonnie Koehler, who got her start as a dialog editor for Ted before moving into picture. Working in transfer was the legendary sound designer Alan Splet, who went on to receive a special Academy Award for his sound effects work on *The Black Stallion*.

I met Ted while working on the Fred Williamson western *Black Rider*, which was being mixed at his studio. Over the years, I brought many films to him because of the quality of work that was being turned out. Ted was willing to wheel and deal, being much more flexible than the more established sound houses like Ryder, Todd AO, Goldwyn, and Glen Glenn. He would often bring in big-time mixers like Don MacDougall and Bob Litt to moonlight on projects.

It was on one of my early mixes with Ted that I learned about "Yellow Sky." I had some scenes where in my inexperience I had not filled in my production tracks as I should have. When we hit the first hole, Ted stopped and looked at me.

"What am I supposed to do with this?" he asked.

"Don't you have a loop or something you can put up?" I questioned desperately.

Ted pressed the intercom to the machine room.

"Put up Yellow Sky," he ordered.

Suddenly I heard a dry desert wind playing. Fortunately, my holes were mostly in exteriors, so Yellow Sky covered my inexperience. The sound effect, which everyone had, was from a Gregory Peck western called *Yellow Sky*. For years it helped inexperienced editors like myself give the impression they knew what they were doing.

The screen in Gomillion's mixing room was huge. I learned very quickly that it was the true judge of editing prowess. On my second feature, *The Devil and Leroy Bassett*, I watched in horror when Reel 11 came up on the screen. It was the big shootout at the climax of the picture, and on the big screen I could clearly see that it was not working. I was smart enough to say to everyone, "Go on to the next reel. I need to take this reel back to the bench."

I saw how to fix it, and after a day of recutting, it was possible to mix the reel and make it play. The important point is that the big screen showed me the error of my ways. One time I got a job revoicing a soft-core nudie voodoo movie. At some point, the police had seized everything and when the court made them return everything, the sound got lost.

Director Don Edmonds hired a group of actors, and we had the shooting script. With Bob Deschaine and my partner Bob McDaniels, we tried to read the actor's lips and relay the dialog. It wasn't easy, and several people from another stage came over and tried to help. I almost destroyed Ted's ADR system when I accidentally backed up past 01:00:00:00.

Nevertheless, through all the trials and tribulations, Ted Gomillion mentored me and taught me about sound. I am very grateful. The lessons I learned from him I still use today.

As at Corman, you could move up, although maybe not quite as fast. When I met Terry Eckton, she was Ted's receptionist. Next, she was in charge of the sound effects library, and fairly soon she was cutting sound. She went on to do many projects at Skywalker Sound.

Ted provided a full package of sound. You could deliver the film to him, and he would provide all the sound editing, recording, and mixing. He had teams working upstairs building effects and finessing dialog. He would hire sound editors at a fixed price per reel to prepare reels for the mix. A young sound editor could always get a job from Ted.

Ted retired in 1988 and set up a company for combining cinematic images with classical music, which was his passion. He talked to me about shooting images to *Grand Canyon Suite*. Before anything came of it, Ted passed away. He left a legacy in the techniques he perfected and in the many creative people he gave a start to as well as his sons, Jeff and Tim, who followed him into the business.

Roger Corman is still alive, but the schools that both Roger and Ted created no longer exist. They were a wonderful way for the new filmmakers to get started and gain experience, and since it was in the real world, it meant something. I don't know of anything like it today and my advice to anyone who asks how to get started is, "Make a movie." You may lose all your money, but you'll get a real education.

I was asked to edit a movie being directed by a secretary at Paramount. When I met her I said, "If you make this film, you will be blued, screwed, and tattooed, and you'll end up in bankruptcy." She replied, "I don't care. It's my dream." I said, "If it's your dream, then I'm in." She made the movie, which I edited, and much of the above happened. But she had her movie and she had her dream, and dreams are what we do.

Chapter 19

American Cinema Editors

E diting is often referred to as the "invisible art." That is because if a film is well edited, the cuts should rarely call attention to themselves. Editors work alone in little rooms and, except for directors and producers, no one knows what they do. Although it is the single process that defines motion pictures as an art form, it has been a mystery to almost everyone. When learning of my profession, people often say, "Oh, you cut out the bad parts." I reply, "No, I put together the good parts."

Because of the invisibility of their craft, two Paramount Studio film editors, Jack Ogilvie and Warren Low, decided to do something about it. At the Masquers Club on October 26, 1950, they met with fellow editors George Amy, Folmar Blangsted, James Clark, Frank Gross, Richard Heermance, William Hornbeck, Fred Knudtson, William Lyon, Fredrick Smith, Richard Van Enger, and Hugh Winn to discuss forming an organization to promote the craft. It was decided to hold a charter membership meeting on November 28, 1950, which was attended by 108 of Hollywood's top film editors.

On January 9, 1951, the first general membership meeting was held, and Donn Hayes suggested the name American Cinema Editors. It stuck, and ACE began appearing after members' names. The organization's credo is as follows: "The objectives and purposes of the American Cinema Editors are to advance the art and science of the editing profession; to increase the entertainment value of motion pictures by attaining artistic pre-eminence and scientific achievement in the creative art of editing; to bring into close alliance those editors who desire to advance the prestige and dignity of the editing profession."

The purpose was to make the "invisible art" visible. The organization began holding ACE roundtables with other industry groups and started a Visiting Editor Program, wherein editors would lecture to film classes at various universities. They produced two films: *Basic Principles of Film Editing*, which has three editors separately editing the same *Gunsmoke* dailies, and *Interpretations and Values of Film Editing*, demonstrating how coverage enhances a scene.

On March 14, 1951, the first ACE Awards Dinner was held to honor the Academy nominees in film editing. In 1962 the group began giving out its own awards, and the ACE Awards tradition began. The *Cinemeditor* magazine began in May 1951. It was during my assignment at Lookout Mountain in the Air Force in 1965 that I first became aware of the magazine and the organization. Donn Hayes, ACE, who had named the group, told me about it.

The name "Eddie" was coined in 1965, and Robert Wise became the first Golden Eddie recipient in 1967. In 1988, ACE initiated its annual Career Achievement Award to honor editors for their contribution to film editing.

I first attempted to join ACE when I was working on *The Winds of War* in 1981. My two sponsors were George Watters, ACE, and Peter Zinner, ACE. I was not accepted for membership at that time. I reapplied in 1988 with Danny Cahn, ACE, and Bud Hayes, ACE, as my sponsors. At that time, I was accepted.

I made the mistake of wandering into the ACE office one day when it was located at Warner Hollywood Studios, the old Doug Fairbanks Studio. George Grenville, ACE, was president, and he put me to work stuffing envelopes for a mailing. That was the beginning of my involvement with ACE.

George had pulled ACE away from a management company that had been running it and was trying to revitalize the organization. He and Bernie Balmuth, ACE, were also suing CableAce for stealing our acronym. It was a David and Goliath battle, with ACE being the underdog, but we won.

At an annual meeting, I was nominated for the board of directors and actually ended up being elected. The board was a real education for me, and I got a lesson in politics. When Michael Hoggan, ACE, became president, he appointed me treasurer after George Grenville resigned.

During this time, the *Cinemeditor* magazine had all but disappeared. George had tried to keep it alive by distributing a small Xerox called *The Trim Bin*. Michael Hoggan continued with it, and on occasion he asked me to write for it, which I enjoyed doing. He appointed me editor, and we began the revitalization of the old magazine.

In an upset election, Tom Rolf, ACE, became president, and I chose not to run again as treasurer. Prior to this, Hoggan and I had hired Laura Young to run the office. Previously, women who had worked for us had been treated like secretaries, often being asked to type up personal things for members. I suggested that we do what Ron Kutak had done at the Editor's Guild. Ron was hired as the business manager, but he changed his title to executive director. We hired Laura Young as the first executive director of ACE. Tom Rolf encouraged Laura and me to try to expand the magazine. We started by selling ads.

This was the 1990s, and Avid and Lightworks were competing for the Hollywood market. We called up one of them and said that the other was buying an ad. Then we called the other and told them the same. They both bought ads, and we were off and running. Any success I achieved with the magazine was because of the guidance of Laura Young.

Danny Cahn, ACE, was always leading me to stories and often writing some of his own. He was a great resource. I convinced Bonnie Koehler, ACE, to write a column called The Cutting Room Floor. Many people approached me with their stories of filmmaking.

Over the next few years, we were able to build up the magazine to where it was a formidable periodical. At the same time, Tom Rolf was formalizing the ACE Educational Center, which had been the brainchild of George Grenville. We managed to work it out with both organizations having matching boards, so it was essentially one group wearing two hats. This was done to prevent friction between the two organizations. ACE was a nonprofit C6, and the Education Center was a C3 charitable organization, which allowed people to contribute to it and get a tax write-off.

During this time when I was not on the board, I still attended board meetings. I remember the night when I joined ACE and saw the board turn over in a few minutes. At that annual meeting, people were nominated and elected to the board immediately. If you weren't at the meeting, you didn't have a vote. I had my picture taken with the new president while I was getting my membership plaque, but the plaque was signed by the old president. I thought there was a better way.

I got together with board member Daniel Cahn, ACE, son of Danny Cahn, and we discussed this. I suggested that we hold elections, like the Editor's Guild did. At the meeting, nominations would be taken and then nominees could mail out campaign statements and everyone could vote through the mail. Daniel proposed it at the next meeting, and we were able to get it into the bylaws.

Figure 19.1. Cinemeditor magazine 2000. (Photo courtesy of American Cinema Editors)

I told Tom Rolf that we should have a ceremony in which we would seat the new board. He agreed, and we had the first Inaugural Reception at the Musicians Local in Hollywood. After that, Pivotal Post began hosting the event, which continues to this day.

During this time, the Board was very active. Bill Gordean, ACE, created the ACE Internship Program, which is ably run by Lori Coleman, ACE, and Diana Friedberg, ACE. It is one of ACE's finest achievements. Daniel Cahn, ACE, and Doug Ibold, ACE, created the corporate sponsorship for the ACE Eddie Awards to keep the event solvent. Many members achieved many things.

Laura Young moved on to other things. She placed an ad in the Hollywood Reporter and we hired Lilli Barsha, granddaughter of former ACE President Leon Barsha, and Jenni McCormick as her assistant. A few weeks later Lilli told me she could only continue in the job if we bought her medical insurance. It was not an unreasonable request, but ACE's finances at the time were not up for it. I told Lilli I would meet her at lunch and accept her resignation.

At that meeting, Lilli suggested we consider Jenni as her replacement. Several people felt Jenni was too young and lacked the academic credentials to be executive director. She was newly married, and I asked her if she could survive without the insurance. She said she could. I saw something in Jenni's character that convinced me she was a winner. Ignoring advice, I hired Jenni with the approval of the board.

In those early days I was concerned that Jenni would grow bored with the job and quit. She told me she had a history of changing jobs. A wonderful thing happened as time went on: Jenni fell in love with ACE and the members. I left the board and pursued other things, but fortunately Jenni remained, and it's been twenty years.

Figure 19.2. Author Jack Tucker receives the Robert Wise Award from Robert Wise himself. (Photo by Peter Zachary and courtesy of American Cinema Editors)

Jenni has far surpassed the career of Georgi Marcher, who held ACE together for many years when the organization operated out of her garage in Los Feliz. Jenni thanked me for hiring her and giving her a career. I reminded her that she had done the same for me. It was Jenni who sent me to California State University, Northridge to teach a course on editing. That led to my career in teaching.

It was a symbiotic relationship, and we as members are so lucky to have Jenni's guidance, insight, and skill. Recently she moved our office to Paramount Studios where ACE actually began in 1950, with Jack Oglvie and Warren Lowe deciding to illuminate the "invisible art." Let's hope Jenni will guide us for another twenty years and beyond.

In 2000 I received the first-ever Robert Wise Award for my work on the magazine. The award was the inspiration of Bonnie Koehler, ACE, and Danny Cahn, ACE. It has been given several times since, but I am the only one to have received it directly from the hands of Robert Wise.

Since leaving *Cinemeditor*, I have seen it grow and flower under the management of others. Before every Oscar night, ACE, along with the Editor's Guild, holds a seminar, Invisible Art/Visible Artists, at the Egyptian Theater in Hollywood. All the editing nominees gather to show clips and talk about their projects. It is a great resource for students and a chance for them to meet real editors.

Credits

Fig. 19.1: Copyright © by American Cinema Editors (ACE). Reprinted with permission.
Fig. 19.2: Copyright © by American Cinema Editors (ACE). Reprinted with permission.

Chapter 20

Shogun and The Pony

The story goes that a cowboy was riding across the prairie when he encountered an Indian busily digging through a large pile of horse excrement. The cowboy asked the Indian what he was doing. The Indian replied, "With this much horseshit, there has to be a pony somewhere."

Now this may sound like a silly analogy, but it is what we in the editing business do: we look for the pony. As I have stated, Tom Rolf, ACE, said, "All movies are really four movies: The movie imagined, the movie written, the movie directed and the movie edited." In each movie, the material changes because of the contribution of the artists; it evolves into something new and original.

When a first cut of a film is made, we are at a starting point. What was imagined and written may not work as well as it did on paper. At this point, we come to the most creative moment in the editing process: finding the movie. Like the pony buried under the excrement, in the first cut there is a movie trying to get out.

Paramount Pictures originally hired me to cut a promo of the *Shogun* miniseries then being edited by four editors. It was the big project of the time. Associate producer Kerry Feltham was in charge of putting the promo together. We started with certain sequences that were needed. Under Kerry's direction, I cut them together, and we eventually arrived at a 17-minute cut that everyone was happy with.

Part of the contract on *Shogun* was that the studio had to deliver two features in addition to the miniseries; one was for Japan and one was for England. Eric Bercovici, the writer/producer, had written a script for the English feature. The Japanese one was merely a cut-down from the 12-hour miniseries. For the English one, some connective scenes had been shot to cover portions of the story not to be shown in the feature. The English feature was not playing.

Kerry felt that he and I could do a better job. He picked a sequence and showed me how to condense to a more efficient cut. We showed it to producer Eric Bercovici and director Jerry London. They were suitably impressed. They fired James Heckert, who was editing the feature, and I got the job.

They ran the picture for me, and I saw the problem. There was nothing wrong with Heckert's editing; in fact, it was good. What was needed was looking beyond the box. The problem was with the script itself. All effort had gone into the 12-hour miniseries, and the feature was treated merely as a necessary contractual delivery requirement. Bercovici felt that it would be impossible to condense the 12 hours into two. He had decided to concentrate on the love story between Blackthorne, the English pilot, and his Japanese interpreter, Mariko.

Having recently read the novel, I felt the love story was not that important. The thing of interest to me—and I hoped the English—was the plotting of the Catholics and of the Japanese warlords. More important was the relationship between the two pilots, Blackthorne and Rodrigues. They were on opposite sides, but like skilled craftsmen, they respected each other as pilots. There was a bond between them that was important to the story.

This relationship as pictured below was significant in that because of their shared craft these two men became friends though politically they would always be enemies. In this scene Blackthorne tries to learn more from Rodrigues, but Rodrigues is unwilling to do so and refers to him as "Enemy." Twice Rodrigues tries to kill Blackthorne and once he saves him. When Blackthorne thwarts the second attempt on his life Rodrigues laments that life was so simple before they met and now, "…there's a hole in the world."

Figure 20.1. Bonds formed between Blackthorne and Rodrigues (1980),
Paramount Pictures.

At that point, I threw the feature script away and asked to see the miniseries. With my then assistant, Maureen O'Connell, we went through the entire 12 hours, after which I dictated what scenes I wanted for the feature. I noted that with commercials removed, *Shogun* only ran about nine hours. Of that nine hours, I would say that perhaps half of the scenes talked about the previous scene; if you removed that, you were down to about four and one half hours. This made achieving a two-hour version seem a little more possible.

In the miniseries as well as the book, Blackthorne's crew plays a part. In Bercovici's feature script, they were totally eliminated. I realized that this was a problem. Much of the book is about Blackthorne becoming Japanese and civilized, as opposed to the barbaric European he had been. There is a scene later in the story, after Blackthorne has become a samurai, when he visits his crew and is disgusted by their filth. It clearly shows the arc of Blackthorne's character. That had to be in the movie; so, the crew had to stay.

Over a period of months, we were able to create a version that played rather well. We were limited to a two-hour format, so some portions played rather quickly and were not allowed to develop as much as I would have liked. We finished the picture, and the studio was happy with it. As a courtesy, we allowed the Japanese, who were doing their three-hour version with Bill Luciano cutting it, to see it. After viewing our version, they scrapped what they had been cutting and took our version as the backbone of theirs. They added many Japanese sequences which I had chosen not to use because we were cutting for a European audience.

James Clavell, who had written the novel, really liked the new version. All during the editing, he would come up to me and ask how the picture was coming. Usually, I would be walking around the lot at night and would feel his presence. His car would silently pull up next to me, and he would ask the inevitable question. I would answer, "It's coming along well, Mr. Clavell. It's all there." "Of course it's all there," he would reply. "I wrote it." Yes, it was there, but I found that pony among the many hours of the miniseries.

One of the scenes I was dealing with in my editing was the earthquake scene in which Blackthorne saves Lord Toranaga. It was a standard Hollywood version of an earthquake, with the ground collapsing and people being buried, but I thought it lacked punch. Kerry Feltham told me that the first time they had attempted to shoot the scene,

Figure 20.2. The redesigned Earthquake (1980), Paramount Pictures.

the dynamite had gone off, but the trenches had not collapsed as planned. There was chaos, but nothing happened. I asked if there was footage of this. He said there was.

We pulled the footage of the first attempt, and I discovered great footage of the horses getting nervous and running wild. I recut the sequence using the horses to start the action off, and it looked more authentic. The still gives some indication of the chaos unleashed in the first attempt at the stunt. It worked so well that the miniseries editors were told to conform their version to match mine, which did not make me popular with them.

If I could have three and a half hours to tell the story, I believed I could really make the film shine. I was told that I was restricted to two hours—so two hours it would be. For over 20 years, in the back of my mind I still wanted that longer version. At the end of my teaching semester one spring, a student came to me wanting to learn more. Layne Hurley wanted to work with me over the summer. I had nothing to cut, and then I remembered *Shogun*. I decided we should try to create the version I had always wanted, using the feature version and the miniseries. We began by loading the feature into the Avid, and then I selected scenes I wanted to incorporate from the miniseries. I had a pretty good idea how the first two hours should play.

The relationship between Blackthorne and Rodrigues was what I wanted to build up. To me, that was the real drama: two craftsmen who respected each other. Rodrigues realizes that Blackthorne is a threat to the exploitation of Japan by the Portuguese. In a storm at sea, he tries to dump Blackthorne into the sea, but fails. Later, Rodrigues is knocked overboard and Blackthorne saves him. Thus begins a love/hate relationship that runs the length of the story and creates much of the drama. Many of these scenes were missing, and I reincorporated them into my longer version.

Another important moment occurs when Blackthorne receives a pheasant from one of his servants. The Japanese, who did not eat meat at that time, want him to prepare and eat it immediately, but he wants to hang it and let it ripen. The Japanese servants are horrified and draw lots as to who will cut the pheasant down and bury it. Because the man who does this has disobeyed Blackthorne, he must commit seppuku and kill himself. He slices his belly open and his second cuts off his head.

When Blackthorne hears of this, he is horrified. He calls the servant girl, who tells him and he calls her, "… a murdering bitch!" He goes up on a hill and stands weeping because he realizes he does not really understand these people. It is an emotional moment and important to Blackthorne's character arc. By adding this moment, it very much personalizes the experience for the viewer. Writer/producer Bercovici never intended this for the feature version, but as the editor, I felt the need for it.

As Blackthorne holds her in his arms he expresses his realization of the great separation between him and the Japanese. He may be Samurai, and he may learn the language, but he will never be Japanese.

When I ran the long version for director Jerry London, he suggested some improvements and volunteered to take a DVD copy to Paramount to suggest putting it out as

Figure 20.3. In an emotional moment, Blackthorne realizes he doesn't understand the Japanese (1980), Paramount Pictures.

the "director's restored version," but the studio had no interest in putting any money into it. The few people who have seen this feel it's the best version; a middle ground, at three and a half hours, between the two-hour feature and the 12-hour miniseries.

The point of this is I finally found my pony, the film that was trying to get out from all the material on *Shogun*. It was not in the conception, the writing, or the directing. It was in the editing room—again, as God and DeMille intended. I have not given up on somehow getting the long version distributed, but even if it never happens I have the satisfaction of achieving my goal.

Chapter 21

MGM and the "Jessie Wars"

I was out of work for fourteen months after Dan Curtis fired me for the second and final time on *The Winds of War*. I couldn't get a job to save my life. No one wanted me. I couldn't get arrested. I took up jogging and drinking, and joined a writer's workshop with a former girlfriend of mine. None of these pursuits inspired me, but they filled the time.

I got a call from an old friend of mine, Ray Guttman, who operated a film coding service. He told me he had a kid working for him who had a half-made sci-fi movie that needed an editor. Ray said he wanted me to cut together what had been shot. He said he could pay me $200 a week. That was not a sum I was accustomed to working for, but it was work.

The kid was Fred Olen Ray and the film was *Biohazard*. Fred offered me Miriam L. Preissel as an assistant. We went to work on the footage, and in a few weeks, we had sequences that we could shop around. Miriam picked up the essentials of editing quickly and went on to become a successful editor. We showed the footage around to distributors without much luck. They liked the editing but weren't hot for the film. At this point, I learned a valuable lesson.

When you're working, you're in demand. When you're out of work, you'll never get a job. I had a job, modest that it was, and suddenly I got a call to come to work on an HBO documentary about *Time* magazine called *The Time of Our Lives*. I could do no more on *Biohazard*, so I went to work on the doc for considerably more money. Miriam eventually finished the film.

Working on this documentary was like a time machine for me. The assistants had all of this stock footage covering much of the twentieth century. I had a script to follow, and as I needed footage, it would be brought to me for viewing on a KEM. I watched the subways being dug in New York. I saw the doughboys come home from World War I and the rise of Adolf Hitler. When I got to the sixties and began viewing the Kennedy footage, I started crying. I sat alone in the editing room sobbing my heart out for all the hopes and dreams we had felt that were now gone and forgotten with the sixties.

As the project was finishing up I got a call from Eric Bercovici, the producer of *Shogun*. I had stayed behind at Paramount to edit *The Winds of War* instead of going to MGM with him to do *The Chicago Story* and *McClain's Law*. He had forgiven me and wanted me to edit a pilot for him called *Jessie*. It was to star Lindsay Wagner, who had the highest TVQ—television desirability—that there was. We were guaranteed to be on the air.

I drove over to the MGM lot in Culver City to meet with Eric. He gave me the script and told me the story. Lindsay was to play a police psychiatrist hunting a serial killer. Tony Lo Bianco was playing opposite her as Lt. Ascoli. The story was set in Tucson, and they were going to shoot two weeks of location there. I would stay behind at the studio and edit. Dick Michaels was the director, and I would have a second editor, Dick Lane, to help me. I asked Ruth Bird, who had assisted me on *The Winds of War*, to assist me on the pilot.

I was very excited to be working for MGM. Known as the greatest studio in the world, it was formed in 1924 by Metro Pictures, Sam Goldwyn's company, and Louie B. Mayer's Mayer Pictures. Goldwyn departed and went his own way leaving the running of the studio to Mayer and the youthful "boy wonder" Irving Thalberg. Under the banner Metro Goldwyn Mayer, some of Hollywood's finest films had been created. Their lineup of talent was impressive. "More stars than in the heavens," they claimed.

Figure 21.1. Lindsay as Jessie and Tony as Lt. Ascoli in the pilot for Jessie.

Originally, most of Culver City had been the studio. There were seven actual lots, but over the years the studio has shrunk to the one main lot. All the same, I was thrilled to work for the studio that had Clark Gable, Spencer Tracy, Judy Garland, and Mickey Rooney under contract.

The night before principle photography was to begin, Eric Bercovici got a call from the network.

"Why are you going to Arizona?" they asked.

Eric replied, "Open your script to page one. Fade In, Tucson, Arizona."

"We thought you would film that in San Fernando Valley."

"Nope. Tucson."

They began shooting in Tucson, and the film rolled in. With two of us editing, we were cut to camera every day in four hours. The two weeks of location went quickly, and soon the company was back at the studio. A police station set was created on one of the stages, and out near Magic Mountain in the Santa Clarita area the exterior of Jessie's house was built.

We continued being cut to camera in four hours. Afterwards, I would go up to the stage and watch Dick Michaels direct. It was great to watch as the scenes were shot, and I knew what was coming in the dailies. I would walk out with the scenes already cut in my mind and ready to attack them in the editing room.

The Alley Cat Bistro opened shortly after I came to Culver City. I met the owners and as it was nearby I began taking my lunch there. After leaving there one day, I encountered an old friend who was now writing for the local newspaper. A couple days later I read in his column, "Lindsay Wagner and Jack Tucker seen noshing at the Alley Cat Bistro." It was true except we were at opposite sides of the restaurant and definitely not together.

On the last day of filming we arranged for the lab to have our dailies ready on Saturday morning. Dick and I cut the last sequences together and inserted them in the cut, and then we all went into a screening room. The picture played pretty well. Dick Lane was let go and I went into the editing room with Dick Michaels where we spent three days improving the film.

I was delegated to take the film to New York to run for ABC. I arrived in Manhattan and checked into the Sheraton Hotel. The film was going to run the next day. I could not be present at the screening but could show up in the morning to check the film out. It was good that I did because there was some confusion about the leaders. The film ran successfully, and we were picked up for series.

Back in Culver City we got ready to go into production for the series. Bercovici wanted me to find two other editors to do the shows with. He had decided, if only to annoy MGM, that each editor would be the associate producer of his or her episode. In addition to getting paid as editors, we would each receive an additional $200 per week for producing. He felt that the three editors would have to work together as a team and help each other out because of a demanding delivery schedule.

I immediately thought of Andy Chulack. I had met Andy when he assisted Danny Cahn, and under his mentorship he'd moved up to editor. Andy was currently editing the hit television series *Cheers*. It took some talking to convince him to leave a hit series and come with us on something that was unknown, but eventually he agreed to join us.

We still needed a third editor to work with Andy and me. We put out the word, and Eric and I interviewed many applicants. My criterion was that the editor had to be recommended by someone that I or Andy trusted and that they have television series experience. We needed someone fast, someone who could deliver a playable version on the first cut that would need only minimal changes.

Eventually we settled on a Steven Brown and hired him. More difficult was hiring Deborah Goodwin as out postproduction coordinator to liaison between we three associate producers. I had met Deborah on *The Winds of War*, where she was working for a company doing promos on the project for ABC. We had become friends, and I was impressed with her work.

MGM told me that to hire her I first had to interview every secretary on the lot who wanted the job. I did this but still wanted Deborah. MGM insisted that I hire one of their people. Frustrated, I went to Eric's partner Dick St. Johns and complained. He got on the phone to human resources and demanded that they hire Deborah. They hired her.

The word came down from the network that they didn't like Tucson. They wanted the story to take place in L.A. but not identified as L.A. This meant reshooting certain scenes for the pilot. Originally, a body had been found in the desert, and that scene wouldn't work for L.A. I was assigned to go around with the location manager and find a new sight for the body to be found. We settled on a site in East Los Angeles, and the director, Dick Michaels, approved it. I rode there in a bus full of extras to watch the scene being shot.

I pointed out to Eric and his partner Dick that in many scenes the uniformed cops had insignias on their uniforms that said Tucson. Wardrobe made new uniforms without Tucson on it. I went through the movie and made a list of shots that had to be remade. Fortunately, Tony Lo Bianco, Lindsay's costar, played Lt. Ascoli, a detective who didn't wear a uniform.

Mostly we had to reshoot portions of scenes and not the whole scene. I had a KEM sent up to the stage, so we could review the material before shooting. I would gather the actors around and run the sequence so they could match the intensity of their performances. It was painful, but we managed to do it. I could also cut in new closeups without the troublesome Tucson insignia.

While I was working on this I got a call from Chiho Adachi, Eric's assistant. She told me that Celeste Holm, the actress who played Lindsay's mother, wanted to meet me. I told Chiho to send her over. She arrived, and I introduced myself and asked what I could do for her.

"I heard you were a nice person, and I just wanted to meet you," Celeste cooed.

Figure 21.2. The troublesome uniforms with the Tucson patch.

"Really? Where did you hear that?" I asked.

"Oh, at a party."

"What party?"

She couldn't say, but as we talked I began to realize she was trying to manipulate me. I remembered that when I was cutting a scene between Lindsay and Celeste, every time I wanted to cut to a close-up of Lindsay, Celeste would do a little mismatch that would force me to cut to Celeste first.

At first, I thought it was accidental, but by the second and third time I saw this was planned. I began to realize that Celeste knew more about editing that I did. Sometimes actors give you a lesser performance in a master to try to force you to use their close ups. This woman went far beyond that. She was subtle and thoroughly understood how I would have to cut the scene.

Celeste asked me if I knew editor Barbara Maclean over at 20th Century Fox. I knew of her as Darryl F. Zanuck's favorite editor who had been with him since the founding of the studio in 1935. She said Barbara was a good friend of hers. Celeste had been in many big films at that studio, including the much-honored *Gentlemen's Agreement* and *All About Eve*. I guessed she learned editing from Barbara.

I was sent to the scoring stage to supervise the recording of the music for the pilot. I didn't have any experience with this, but John LaSalandra, who had been music editor on *Shogun*, was there to guide me. We had a new composer who was just starting out named Alan Silvestri and who would become famous with *Back to the Future*. We

Figure 21.3. Celeste Holm teaching the author editing.

assembled on the stage with a seventy-six-piece studio orchestra. I was told that in the old days this stage was kept busy fifty-two weeks a year knocking out scores.

The movie was playing on a big screen behind the orchestra. It was a black and white dupe cued for where the music began and ended. Silvestri cleverly let Harry, the head of the music department, conduct. A cue would come up, and the orchestra would play. At the end of the piece everyone would turn to me.

LaSalandra said, "If you don't like it, we can change it."

"No, no. It's great. Let's move on." What the hell did I know.

It was an excellent score, but we were the only ones to hear it; it was never used. A new score was written when David Gerber came on.

One of our first episodes was to be directed by Jackie Cooper and edited by Andy. As he wasn't on salary yet, I accompanied Cooper on the scouting for the film. He explained to me how he wanted to see his dailies. It was essentially the way we always did it at MGM. We went in script order and showed the master first, followed by the next widest shot and working down to the close-ups. Regardless of which order the dailies were shot, we built them in this manner. This way it was easy to see if the scene was properly covered. We began shooting the series.

I got to work with a number of directors on the series, my favorites being Joel Oliansky and Corey Allen. Corey was an ex-actor. He had played Buzz in *Rebel Without a Cause* in the famous "chickey run," scene where he and James Dean race toward a cliff to see who is chicken. Corey was a delight as a person but not so much in the cutting room. He had a formula. If an actor exited screen right, in the next scene the actor had to enter screen left. He also liked longer pacing. I showed him a cut that was within 30 seconds of time, and when he finished with it we were five minutes over. Nevertheless, Corey was a splendid guy, and I liked working with him.

One day we ran into each other at the MGM gate.

"I'm directing the next episode," he said. "Are you cutting it?"

"No," I replied. "I think it's Andy."

Corey looked at me wistfully.

"Oh, well. We're both young," he said.

A growing hostility between Eric Bercovic and Lindsay Wagner was developing. Eric was told by the network that we were an action series, and Lindsay, after having been injured on *The Bionic Woman*, would not do action. In the pilot, she was seated next to Tony Lo Bianco in a car chase. Eric had written the series for Tucson so he would not have to deal with her. Before each episode, we would have a meeting to go over the script. Lindsay's mother, who acted as her manager, would attend these and so would I. After each scene, we would look to Mother and she would say, "Lindsay will do it."

Lindsay was unhappy with some of the scripts. When she arrived on the set, she would often have new pages for the scene she had hired someone to write. The problem was the new pages were based on previous versions of the script that had already been updated. It made for much confusion. Eric would not discuss these things with her, and their relationship became decidedly icy.

Lindsay sent Eric a potted plant as a peace offering. He took the plant and hurled it out the window, bouncing it off her building. I spoke to Eric and pointed out that Lindsay was the only person on the show that they would not fire. She had the TVQ. "The rest of us are expendable," I said. MGM fired Eric and replaced him with David Gerber. Bruce Pobjoy, MGM's post supervisor, told Gerber to keep the editors because they knew the material. Unfortunately, he fired Deborah Goodwin too. I told Eric I was going to stay on the show.

"You can afford to be fired. I can't," I told him. "You're under contract, and you're paid even if you're not working. I do not have that advantage. Maybe I can save something of what we did." We all stayed on.

We all lost our associate producer jobs, and Chris Chulack, Andy's cousin, was brought in as associate producer. Gayle Mnookin, one of the women I had interviewed, was made postproduction coordinator. Gerber brought in David Wages, an older editor, to help us. He was assisted by Darrell Upshaw, who was African American and had been hired as part of affirmative action.

Some of the editors resented Darrell, but we were all grateful a few weeks later, when Wages had a heart attack. Darrell jumped in and administered CPR until the medics came. He saved Wages life. Afterwards I asked him, "Where did you learn that?"

"I saw it on TV," he replied.

"Darrell, when you assist me, don't ever let me out of your sight."

Soon I found myself back on the second reshoot of the pilot. Dick Michaels had turned down directing it, but Corey Allen agreed to it. The script girl and I stayed with

Figure 21.4. Lindsay Wagner and Bill Lucking during a reshoot for the Jessie pilot.

him because by now everyone, including Lindsay, was thoroughly confused. We would tell him which angles he could shoot for new material Gerber had added.

One night we were going down Washington Boulevard in Culver City, towing Lindsay and Tony Lo Bianco doing a driving shot. At the head of our procession was a traffic cop clearing the way. We followed with a truck towing the actors, followed by a crew car blocking out the cop who was at the back end. Corey, the script girl, and I were all mounted on the truck perched over the towed car.

Suddenly, our procession came upon someone driving ahead of us. He saw the cop and panicked. He stopped suddenly, not knowing what to do. This forced the truck towing the car to stop. I thought all three of us would pitch forward and end up in Lindsay's lap. Fortunately, the truck made a gentle stop.

Because of the many changes we had to make in the pilot, it did not have a standard television running time. It was too long for an hour time slot and too short for ninety minutes. ABC said will take it at whatever length it was. The pilot was scheduled, and we had to satellite it to get it on the air from a separate color-corrected print interlocked with a master-mixed sound track.

Brandon Stoddard, the head of ABC, wanted to see the pilot before it played. I booked a screening room and ran the film for him. It was just the two of us. At one point, Brandon turned to me and said, "I'd like to make a change." I lost it completely; too many versions and too many changes.

"Get on the phone to TV Guide and take the ads out!" I screamed at him. "We won't make the air date!"

"But it's one little change," he protested.

"Eighty people have to make your change," I yelled. "There's music, sound effects, dialog, and mixing. And then there's a new print. We're sending it up to a satellite just to get it on the air now. Forget the change."

Stoddard turned around, thoroughly destroyed by my tirade. I never worked on another ABC show.

Not having scripts ready to shoot, David Gerber grabbed some old scripts from his show *Police Story* and had writers retool them for *Jessie*. The Writers Guild found out about this and were not happy. Somehow it got worked out, and we continued shooting.

We ran the first show I cut for Gerber on a KEM to get notes from David. Ruth took them, and I was full of myself thinking I knew what he wanted. I made the changes over Ruth's objections that I was doing it wrong, which became obvious when Gerber saw them. He sent me back to fix them. This time I listened to Ruth.

When Gerber showed up at the KEM, I said to him, "Boy, this time your notes better be right."

"Be glad you have a sense of humor," Gerber growled.

"No, I'm hoping you do."

This time, the changes were right.

One Friday night I received a list of notes from the network. Bruce Pobjoy wanted me to stay late, make the changes, and show them to Gerber on Saturday. I refused to do it.

"I have read the notes. Half of them David won't do," I said. "I'm not gonna make changes that he will just have me change back. I'll come in tomorrow morning and read him the notes. The ones he wants me to do, I'll do."

I read the notes to Gerber. Most of them he wouldn't do, but every now and then he'd say, "We'll do that one for them. We'll give 'em that one."

Jessie didn't make it. There was too much going against it. Too many people going in different directions. We shot eight episodes; six went on the air before we were cancelled. Lindsay had a party on a boat in Long Beach, intending to burn the script and put it to rest. I did not attend and the captain wouldn't let her light a fire on the boat.

Contractually, the last two episodes had to be finished although no one would ever see them. I finished the last one. It was over. I closed the cutting room door and turned out the lights.

Years later I was eating in Beverly Hills when I noticed Lindsay across the room. Out eyes met for a moment. I think she remembered me but was not sure from where. By her look, I think she realized it was a bad experience.

Chapter 22   *Getting Magnetized*

Getting magnetized is like being possessed by the devil—you need an exorcism. As with all progress, there is a double-edged sword. Originally, we recorded and edited with optical tracks, and we had the advantage in editing to be able to see the sound on the track. It made it easy to locate words when editing. For the sound mixers, it was a sword held over their heads.

To mix to optical track, you have to be very good and very well rehearsed. You go through the reels again and again so you have every cue memorized and every level figured. Once you start recording, you are committed. If you make a mistake, you've ruined a 900-foot piece of film. Do that very often and you won't have a job.

In the late 1940s, recording to magnetic track came about. This was good for the mixers because if they made a mistake, it was only a matter of taking the roll of mag down and degaussing (erasing) it. Then, you could put the roll up again and all that you have lost is time.

The editors weren't that happy with mag because you could no longer see the sound; you had to listen to the track. Also, there was the problem of becoming magnetized. It was easy enough to become magnetized running through equipment and over mag heads. In those days, we still cut the film with scissors and stuck it together with paper clips. Then, the assistant would go through the reel, remove the clips, and glue the shots together on a pedestal hot splicer. As each track splice was made, the assistant would punch a hole with a diamond-shaped punch in the mag track to eliminate any magnetic pop sound.

With the elimination of optical track, we began switching from large pedestal splicers to the small butt splicers. This allowed the editor to do his own splicing as he went along. The butt splicers had originally been used for Cinerama films to reinforce splices because of the incredible amount of torque put on the film. Gradually, they were adopted into mainstream film editing.

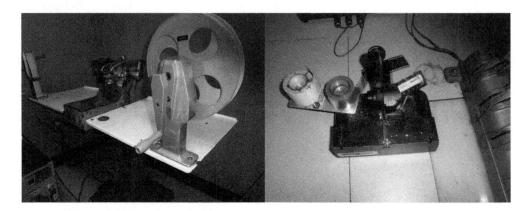

Figure 22.1. (left) Pedestal Hot Splicer (right) Butt Tape Splicer

Regularly, all equipment that came in contact with the mag track had to be degaussed to get rid of any magnetic buildup. This included the sound head on the Moviola, the sound heads on synchronizers, butt splicers, scissors, etc.

When I began editing my first union feature, *Flatbed Annie and Sweetiepie: Lady Truckers*, the producer rented a room for me at a building on La Brea Avenue. It was a large room with carpeting and a couch. I moved in and began editing. Fairly soon, I noticed my splices were popping.

I called the vendor we were renting our equipment from, and he sent a man out to degausse all the equipment. Despite doing this, the popping still continued. Todd AO took my splicers and put them through a huge degausser, but still it persisted. In desperation, I considered a Catholic priest and an exorcism.

That did not become necessary because I discovered that if I removed my shoes and worked in my stocking feet, nothing became magnetized. It was a miracle, so I did not question it. The thought of having to go through and bloop every splice with the diamond punch was more than I could handle. I suppose the carpet was the culprit, and the simple act of removing my shoes negated it. Getting magnetized is one aspect of working on film I do not miss.

Chapter 23

Working in Italy: The Gold Crew

After the demise of *Jessie*, I was out of work at MGM. Eric Bercovici had gone on to Italy to begin prepping for his movie-of-the-week, *The Gold Crew*. Eric's script was from a novel by Frank M. Robinson and Thomas N. Scortia. Their previous effort, *The Glass Inferno*, had been one of two books that formed the basis for the highly successful feature *The Towering Inferno*. The story was about a Trident nuclear submarine that is, because of its nuclear power, the third most powerful country in the world, and in which the crew has become crazy and is going to launch their missiles, starting World War III.

Eric had adapted the novel while we were doing *Jessie* and had MGM's approval to make the film. Since MGM and Eric were not getting along, the studio had underfunded the movie. Bercovici had flown to Rome and made a deal with Italian producers to pick up the overages. The deal was that the film had to be made in Italy and the Italians would get the rights to Europe. Eric was willing to accept an Italian cinematographer, Cristiano Pogany, but he insisted that he needed an American editor. Unfortunately, it wasn't me.

Steven Brown, who I had hired as the third editor on *Jessie*, was going to Italy to cut this for Eric. I was angry because I had hired Brown after going through many lesser applicants who Eric would have taken, and I had kept post running well. Bercovici was impressed with the way Brown had cut a particular episode. It was well-edited but so was what I had done on *Shogun*.

I was at home a few weeks later working in the garden when I got a phone call from Bercovici.

"I'm going to save your career again," he said. "I want you in Rome on the first of August."

"What happened to Steve Brown?" I asked.

"He got a permanent job here in Los Angeles. Call my office, and they'll get you what you need for Italy."

Thirty minutes after calling me, Eric hired Larry Peerce to direct. I had never met him, but I had seen his first feature film, *One Potato, Two Potato*. It was about an interracial marriage between a White woman and a Black man. The woman's first husband returns and sues for custody of their child because he doesn't want the child growing up in a Black family. It was a unique film for the time.

I asked MGM to get me tapes of all of Larry's films. I watched *The Incident, The Other Side of the Mountain, A Separate Peace, The Bell Jar*, and *Two Minute Warning*. I liked Larry's films and was eager to work for him.

I had to go to the Italian consulate, which fortunately was near in Brentwood, and apply for a work permit to be allowed to work in the country. MGM did the paper work. All I had to do was show up and it was granted.

My friend Deborah Goodwin went to the airport with me. On the way, I stopped at MGM to pick up a package for our technical advisor, Captain Bill Graves. Then we proceeded to the VIP lounge for Alitalia at the LAX airport. Because of the union contract, they had to fly me first class, so Deborah and I were having free drinks in the lounge as we waited for my departure.

When the time came, I said goodbye to Deborah as an airline official escorted me to the plane ahead of everyone else. I was ushered aboard in front of the waiting passengers and taken upstairs in the 747 to the first-class cabin. I was the only one in first class.

A steward seated me where I wanted, and the flight took off. It was an over-the-Pole flight to Milan and then on to Rome. The steward asked me when I would like dinner. I told him, and I was given slippers and a sleeping mask. When I was eating, he offered me different wines for the various dishes. Afterwards, he asked if he could start the movie. I said yes and fell asleep as it played.

The steward awakened me as we were going over the North Pole so I could see the Northern Lights. He said it was too bad that I was going to Italy in August when everything is closed while people were on vacation. I explained that I would be staying for six months and wouldn't be going back this year.

The next morning, I was served breakfast before we landed in Milan. After a short stop we flew on down to Rome and I emerged into Fiumicino airport. At customs I was held up when they opened the package for Bill Graves and discovered 8 mm film in it. I could see Maureen O'Connell watching as I was escorted away by security for smuggling film.

In the security area, I talked to a woman who spoke English. I explained that I was an MGM employee coming to work in Rome at Cinecitta Studios. The 8 mm I brought was for a co-worker. She said an import agent from Cinecitta would have to contact security to get the film. I walked out to meet Maureen, who was anxiously waiting for me with Sandro Nardi, a production driver.

"What happened?" she asked. "I thought they were arresting you."

"No, there was some 8 mm film in the box I brought for Captain Graves. I think they thought I was smuggling porno."

Maureen introduced me to Sandro, and we went outside to the car. Apparently, production cars in Europe tended to be Mercedes and so was ours. We loaded my luggage and headed into the city. As we drove along, my eyes were opened wide.

I was coming back to a place I had never been. It all looked so familiar as we made our way into the city. I felt that I had been there, although not in this life. Perhaps I was remembering it from the movie *Roman Holiday*. We pulled through the Piazza del Poppolo and arrived at the Residenzia de Ripetta, where I was to live. Sandro unloaded me and I moved into my room on the second floor, which in Italy is called the first floor.

"We'll be back in a couple of hours to take you to dinner. You should stay up to beat the jet lag," Maureen told me.

My apartment consisted of two rooms: a bedroom and a living room. There was a coffee pot and a hot plate, all the comforts of home. I unpacked and in two hours I received a call from downstairs that my friends were waiting for me in the bar.

I entered the small, lobby bar and found Maureen, Eric Bercovici, his secretary Chiho, and his son Hillary. We had a round of drinks and then went around the corner where we had dinner in a charming little restaurant called La Penne Doca. I had a truly fabulous pepper steak.

I had the weekend to rest up. Shooting began on Monday at a practical location, the Collegio Internazionale S. Lorenzo Da Brindisi, on the outskirts of Rome. It was doubling as a naval hospital where Sam Waterston, playing Commander Renslow, Captain of the Blue Crew, was undergoing medical tests. Our Trident submarine, the *Montana*, was manned by two separate crews that alternated every seventy days: the Blue Crew and the Gold Crew.

In the story, the government has hidden a tape recorder on board the sub to give out messages leading up to a war situation to see if the men under pressure would fire the nuclear missiles. The Gold Crew, captained by David Soul and with Robert Conrad as his executive officer, were to be the guinea pigs. Only they and the ship's doctor, played by Richard Roundtree, knew the messages were part of a drill. Unfortunately, after hiding the tape recorder in the wall, they had painted over it with a fast-drying paint that was toxic.

The toxicity began making the captain and all the crew believe that the drill was real and they were going to go to war with the Russians. Only Robert Conrad was not affected because he was taking a drug for depression and the side effects made him immune. He was trapped on a submarine full of mad men.

The Navy was not particularly inclined to help us on the film due to the fact it was about a disaster that could happen. We did have retired Capt. Bill Graves as a technical advisor, but he was not a submariner. Our production designer was Beala Neel, who had been to the christening of a Trident submarine and been able to tour it. He was to

Figure 23.1. Larry Peerce, Jack Tucker, and Eric Bercovici.

a great extent creating the sub on the stage from memory and from sketches he'd made after the tour.

I was driven to the set to meet our director, Larry Peerce. Eric introduced us, and I suggested that Larry come by the cutting room later in the week and see what I had cut to make sure I was giving him what he wanted. Then I was driven to Cinecitta Studios, at the southern end of Rome. It was very exciting to drive through the gates of the largest studio in Europe. It had been built by Mussolini, and such films as *Quo Vadis*, *Helen of Troy*, *Ben-Hur*, *La Dolce Vita*, and *Cleopatra* had been filmed there.

Since all the cutting rooms were full, we were delegated to a couple of trailers. Maureen was technically my assistant, but she was to move up as soon as we had sufficient footage for two of us to work. Giorgio De Vincenzo was the lead assistant, and he was supported by Patrizia Ceresani, Stefano Moni, Carlo Balestrieri, and Emanuela Lucidi. I met Arthur Fellows, who was the producer under Eric, and Frederick Muller, the associate producer.

For equipment, we had the Prevost flatbed and two or three Moviolas that we had rented from Samuelsons in London. The Italians were used to the Prevost, and the Moviolas were for we Americans. Americans are brought up on the Moviola, which is basically a nonlinear system. Everything is broken down by the shot, viewed on the Moviola, and built through a synchronizer. This makes for a very fast method of cutting, so very necessary for quick turnaround in the studio system.

Figure 23.2. The cutting rooms.

Flatbeds are entirely linear. The editor must scroll back and forth to find the shots he wants and then assemble them for working on the flatbed. It works well for European films, which are more filmmaker driven than studio driven.

The American system is so financially driven that labs operate twenty-four hours a day, 365 days a year. You turn your film in by midnight, and you get your prints in the morning. In Italy, the labs are closed at night. What you shoot on Monday gets processed and printed on Tuesday, and you get it on Wednesday and then only after the director of photography has seen and released it.

So on Wednesday I was able to begin cutting. I cut together the scenes that had been shot with Sam Waterson on the hospital set. It was pretty standard stuff. By Friday I was able to begin on the Command Center footage being shot at the same location. Larry came by and I ran him what was cut. He gave me a few notes and was happy with what he saw. I was giving him what he wanted.

Eric told me in confidence that MGM was planning to shut the film down because they felt it was going to cost too much. He warned me not to tell Larry. I wasn't worried. I knew that an executive from the studio had brought two million dollars cash into Italy and given it to the production. I knew there was no way the Italians would let MGM have that money back.

I remembered in the fifties that Jack Warner had wanted to get the money the studio had earned during the war, and they wouldn't allow it to leave the country. Jack ended up having to make two movies in Italy to use that money. He ended up making *Helen of Troy* and *Land of the Pyramids* in the country.

The second week, the company relocated to a military base at Taranto, down in the heel of the boot of Italy. There they were shooting exteriors of the sub, which was a mock up. They shot going on and off the sub and scenes on the bridge. On Thursday they moved back to Rome and shot Pentagon scenes on Friday.

The Italian way of shooting had to be revamped slightly for our Hollywood production. The Italians do not shoot direct sound. They replace all the dialog so on an Italian set you may hear all manner of noises going on while they are shooting. Hammers may be banging away building sets. Fellini would often hire amateurs if he liked their face and tell them to say something, like the number twenty-eight. Later he would have a professional actor put in the words that he wanted.

We did not have that advantage and had to explain to the crew that there had to be absolute silence during a take. We were going to use the sound recorded by Paul Le Mare on the set. It was because of this we had hired an English sound man instead of an Italian.

I made the mistake of asking Paul Le Mare to join me one night at La Penne Doca for dinner. He sat down and immediately ordered six bottles of wine. I, being a fool, drank them with him. I woke up the next morning still drunk. I rushed to dailies, and while watching them with Larry Peerce, I told him I was drunk and what had happened.

"Oh, Jack," he advised. "You can't drink with the English. They are raised in pubs from the time they are children. No American can keep up."

I knew he was right and was very careful about my drinking around Paul after that.

We were two weeks in and we had a routine going. I would get up around 7:00 a.m. and go to the Borghese Gardens and jog. Then I would return to my room, make coffee, and shower and shave. I would dress and meet Maureen and Chiho near the Spanish Steps. The three of us would board the B line of the subway, which would take us to Cinecitta.

Figure 23.3. Giorgio De Vincenzo, Maureen O'Connell, and Jack Tucker.

Arriving at the studio, we would go into the bar for coffee and toast. We would meet Giorgio there. One day I noticed a tall, distinguished man talking to a gorgeous blonde in the bar. It was Sean Connery. He was doing *The Name of the Rose*. It was particularly exciting since we were all reading that book.

Often in the bar we would see Sergio Leone, who had made Clint Eastwood a star with his "spaghetti westerns." Sergio was a very nice man, and he would listen intently when Robert Conrad would be going on about something even though he did not speak English. Occasionally, we would see the legendary Fellini.

We would usually go to lunch off the lot, but sometimes we would eat in the Mensa where the Italians ate. It was good and it was inexpensive. The problem eating at a restaurant off the lot was it was not quick. Eric called me one day and said, "Jack, no more two hour lunches." I replied, "Thanks. I can't do it in less than three hours."

In the evening, the Americans and the Brits would meet in the bar at the Rezidenzia De Ripetta for drinks, then on to dinner. Much of the office staff was English. Marilyse Morgan was our production coordinator. Supporting her were Janice Munro and Gay Whelan. We would take a cab to whatever restaurant we chose, but we would walk back after dinner. It was a chance to talk and work off the meal.

One night in the bar, I ran into Ben Gazzara. He was in Rome making a film for a Sicilian director. Ben was fascinated with my Malacca walking stick. He would ask about it.

"It's a Malacca, Ben," I would say.

"You say you got it in Malacca," he would reply.

"No, it's the wood. The wood is Malacca."

"You say you got it in Malacca."

Almost every time we met in the bar, we would have this conversation. We had both had a lot to drink so it didn't seem to matter that we'd had the same conversation the night before.

Our crew was rounded out by Gabrielle Tana, the daughter of Dan Tana, the owner of the restaurant that bears his name in Los Angeles. Eric had met her in Yugoslavia on her father's island, and she was eager to join our group. We both lived in the same Residenzia, so we had many dinners together. She ended up working in the production office.

In the mornings we would watch dailies with Larry. We built them MGM style in script order starting with the master shots and then moving in on the coverage. It was easy to tell if we were covered, and usually we were. I would polish the previous day's cutting before lunch. After lunch I would take a half hour nap and then begin a new scene. When I had it cut, I would go home and let it sit over night for polishing the next day.

One day on the submarine set on Stage 1, Larry asked me to shoot some inserts with Robert Conrad of a telegram he was reading. Conrad wanted us to shoot it fast and was annoyed that we took so much time setting up the shot. Then Arthur Fellows joined us and we shot some inserts of the big board in the Command Center. It was fortunate that Giorgio De Vincenzo was there because he made me slate everything.

Personally, I am a stickler for slates. I have often said, "If you don't slate it, don't shoot it. If won't be in the film." Or, "You name your kids so you can remember them. Do the same for your scenes." Shooting with Conrad rattled me, and I just wanted to finish the pickups. Giorgio didn't let me get away with not slating.

In the third week, I began cutting scene 62. It was a dialog scene between Robert Conrad, the executive officer of the Gold Crew, and Richard Roundtree, who played the ship's psychiatrist. It took place in the officer's quarters. The coverage was a master, a pickup master, and over the shoulder and singles on the two men. It looked fine in dailies.

I had my lined script mounted on a music stand next to my Moviola. With one look at the lined script, I knew we were in big trouble. I could see the line for the master shot as it moved down the page and the line for the pickup master, which overlapped it. But all the coverage, the over the shoulder and the singles, began after the master had ended.

Normally when a director stops a master, he backs up three or four lines and starts the pickup master. You cannot directly cut from a master to a pickup master because they are the same shot. It would create a jump cut. You need to go to coverage to transition from one to the other. I realized all this from simply looking at the lined script. We had created a hole in coverage. It was not something we were likely to spot in dailies, but it was painfully obvious looking at the lined script.

I felt that our Italian script supervisor, Marion Mertes, should have immediately caught this at the set but for whatever reason she had missed it. I quickly called the stage and asked to speak to the director. He came on the phone.

"Larry, we've played through a hole," I announced.

"Jack, what are you saying?" he asked.

"On scene 62, there's a hole in the coverage. I can't cross from the master to the pickup. I'll try to see if I can fix it, but we may have to shoot something."

"I'll make tomorrow's call an hour earlier so we can shoot it."

Well, of course, I couldn't fix it. The next morning, we all assembled on Stage 1, the interior submarine set, to shoot a pickup shot with Robert Conrad. We shot Larry's version of the pickup, we shot my version, and we shot Marion Mertes' version. I don't remember which one I used, but it worked well.

I was concerned about the model work that was going to be done on the show. For this type of film we would need shots of the sub doing things. We got a great POV shot of a sub surfacing from MGM's *Ice Station Zebra* that we used to open the film. In the seventh week of filming, the crew moved to the big tank on Malta to shoot underwater sub shots with models and the final sinking of the *Montana*. The underwater model shots were fine, but the surface ones didn't look that good. We ended up using stock shots for most of the surface shots.

While everyone was gone, I made tapes of the dailies so the assistants could continue breaking down the footage so we could keep cutting. By now Maureen had joined me in the editing.

Shortly after the crew had returned to the studio, I received a call from Arthur Fellows.

"Jack, I need to see the film dailies of the days I missed when I was on Malta," Arthur explained.

"I made you a tape. Isn't that enough?"

"No, I can't tell from the tape," he insisted.

"The dailies have been broken down for cutting," I said.

"Well, have the assistants put them back together so I can see them," Fellows insisted.

"I won't do that," I yelled, getting angry. "The assistants are working very hard. They don't have time to do this. The dailies look fine, and I'm not going to have them reassembled just so you can look at them on the big screen." I slammed the phone down.

I later learned from Bill Graves, who was in the production office where Arthur was calling from, that Fellows growled, "No cutter is going to talk to me like that!" Arthur put the phone down and started for the editing trailers.

At the time, I was unaware that Arthur Fellows had once punched out the legendary David O' Selznick. When they were making Selznick's *A Farewell to Arms*, Selznick had grabbed or pushed Fellows, and Arthur turned around and laid the legendary producer out. Thirty years of working for the autocrat had come to a head. Selznick was carried off on a stretcher, and Fellows packed his belongings and left the set. This was the man who was angrily coming to confront my insolence.

Fortunately, by the time that Arthur Fellows had walked across the studio to the editing trailers, both of us had calmed down. He walked in to my cutting room. In a flash I saw a way out for both of us.

"Arthur, why don't I just have the lab reprint the dailies, and you can watch them silent. If you need to hear sound, we can print that up too and sync it."

"That'll work," Arthur exclaimed. "I can live with that." We shook hands, and after that we became friends.

We needed a stock shot of a missile being launched from a Trident sub, and we managed to get one. To make it seem like four missiles were being fired, Arthur devoted himself to adding optical effects to make it seem like different shots.

One afternoon, production called me and said that Yvette Mimieux wanted to see her dailies. She was playing Robert Conrad's love interest. She had always been a heart-throb of mine since I saw her with Rod Taylor in *The Time Machine*. I was excited to meet her. The lab closed at 6:00 p.m., so I had to bribe the projectionist with a bottle of champagne to stay so we could run them. I brought the reels over and waited, but she never showed up and I let the projectionist go home.

Our dialog coach was Mickey Knox. He also played a detective in one of the scenes. He was known to American crews as "the Mayor of Rome." Mickey had been blacklisted during the fifties after starting out on what could have been a distinguished career with Tony Curtis in *City Across the River*. He'd been in Rome for thirty years or so, and whenever an American production showed up, he was hired as the dialog coach and usually played a cop or a reporter. In *The Winds of War*, he had played the Paramount distributor in Rome who warned Ali McGraw to get out of the country.

Mickey was proud of the fact that he lived in a house that Dante had once lived in when he was writing *The Divine Comedy*. When Dan Curtis had been there, Mickey was showing Dan around and Dan asked him, "Who is this Dante you keep talking about?"

We were able to get a submarine officer to show David Soul and some of the actors how our equipment was supposed to work in the control room. David spent a lot of time learning so it was second nature to him when he was doing his scenes.

Key to the story was David going crazy because of the paint fumes. Early in the story, he needed be the strong commander but slowly we needed to see him dissolve into a lunatic. David handled the transition very well with great subtlety, and I did all I could to help him with my choice of shots.

Richard Roundtree presented other problems for me. He was an action hero and the star of the *Shaft* movies. With action he was a natural, but in our film he was playing a psychiatrist. He had to discuss medical terms like *tachycardia* in his dialog scenes. He was not comfortable with these words, so when he started to speak I would cut to the listener and streamline his dialog so it flowed trippingly from his tongue.

We were approaching the time when we were to run our first cut. I was concentrating on finessing the ending, and Maureen was handling everything else. We were

Figure 23.4. David Soul asks Robert Conrad for his support.

supposed to deliver a three-hour movie-of-the-week for NBC and a two-part, four-hour miniseries for the Italians. We decided we would run part one in the morning, have lunch, and then run part two.

Italian theaters are not like American ones. There is no concession stand. Half way through the movie, the film stops and End of Part One is projected on the screen. The lights come on, and vendors come out selling popcorn, candy, ice cream, and drinks. After a short intermission, Part Two continues.

David Gerber back at MGM pointed out that the film was too short to be a two-parter. "How are you going to make up the time?" he asked in a phone conversation. I explained that I would start Part Two with a recap of the first part. As we got close to Part Two, the recap would become longer and longer until it would seamlessly merge into the second part. Gerber was satisfied.

We ran our Part One, and at the dramatic ending a card appeared reading End of Part One appeared on the screen. Eric and Larry got a big laugh out of it. We went across the street for our customary three-hour lunch and then returned to the screening room to watch Part Two. All in all, the film played pretty well.

We did have a slight problem in that we had to deliver the American version first, and they would get the cut negative. The longer Italian version would be a CRI (color reversal internegative). The associate producer Frederick Muller was all ready to start making CRIs of everything, which would have cost a fortune. I had a better Idea.

I said that we should go through the cut Maureen and I had presented and make any changes that were necessary without trying to shorten the film. Then we would have negative cut on this long version and a CRI of that made, which we would put aside as the Italian version. Then we would go through and cut the three-hour American version and finish it. The negative would be recut to match that version. When it was completed, we would get back on the Italian version and finish it.

We went ahead with my plan. Since Eric and Larry were getting along, we decided not to have a director's cut. Instead, the four of us (Eric, Larry, Maureen, and I) would go through it together and slug it out between ourselves. There was no ego involved, and between us we came up with a version that played well and was the correct running time. NBC was going to send an executive to Italy to approve the film.

When the executive arrived, Eric told me he didn't want the fellow making any changes.

"Every time he asks for a change," Eric instructed, "tell him if we do the change we won't be able to deliver on time."

So I did as I was asked. Every time the executive suggested something, I explained why we couldn't do it. Finally, in frustration he said, "I've come all the way over here, and you won't let me do anything. Why am I here?"

We were standing in front of my big production board showing all the scenes from the movie. Looking at it, I was inspired. "Why don't you adjust the act breaks?" I suggested. These were the commercial breaks between portions of film that were

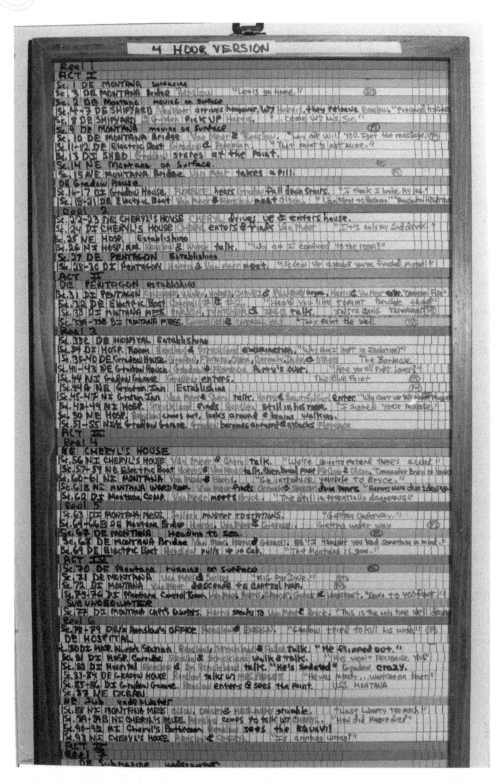

Figure 23.5. The big production board.

predetermined by the network. The executive liked my suggestion. Together we went over the production board, and I would move the act breaks where he wanted them. He went away satisfied.

About this time, we received word from MGM and NBC that they wanted to change the name to *The Fifth Missile*. In their wisdom, they decided that nobody knew what *The Gold Crew* meant. I didn't think the new title was any improvement, and it didn't convey the excitement inherent in the original title.

Getting the negative cut was a big deal. Fellini had something cutting, and he had priority. Giorgio and I worked out an act to speed up our negative cutters. We would walk over to where these women were cutting our negative. Giorgio would scream and yell at them while I stood there and wrung my hands looking very worried. Afterwards, we would go to the bar and have coffees. We repeated this every day, and the negative got cut.

It was time to start cutting sound effects for the American version. We wanted an English sound editor to lead the team. Giorgio, Maureen, and I looked through the Kemps book for sound editors. We considered Winston Ryder, who had worked for David Lean, but eventually we settled on Graham Harris and brought him down from England.

About this time, Giorgio and our apprentice editor, Emanuela Lucidi, came to see me. She was almost in tears. I learned that Frederick Muller was letting her go from our crew. There was no apparent reason for it, and to make matters worse, he was her uncle. Giorgio told me, "Go talk to him, Jack. He's afraid of you. Tell him we want Emanuela."

I got all fired up and went marching over to see Frederick in the production office. I told him in no uncertain terms that I wanted Emanuela on our crew. He backed down, and we assigned her to the sound editing crew.

I returned to editing with the good news. Giorgio suggested we go somewhere special for lunch, so we piled in his car and drove south. We came to a little town on the crest of a cliff overlooking a valley below. The view was magnificent. I looked out at the vista from the cliff and knew how much I loved Italy. Giorgio and I split the cost of the lunch for our crew.

We hired Pino Donaggio to score the picture, and Lizabeth Gelber came on as our music editor. Lizabeth, like Giorgio, was totally bilingual, which make it easy to work with her. We moved forward to the mix, which we were going to do on the lot. Danilo Sterbini was our rerecording mixer.

The mix went well despite certain problems where things were lost in translation. We were scheduled to go up to London to make the air tape for NBC. We were all warned not to tell customs that we were there to work. Without a work permit, we would be arrested, so we all claimed we had finished a picture in Italy and were in England for a vacation.

We checked into the Atheneum Hotel and had dinner. They had a unique bar with all the single-malt scotches on the wall. According to Eric, the story was that if you tried a drink from each of the single malts, they would give you a bottle of the one you preferred. Aside from the fact that you would have spent a fortune trying all of them, it would have taken forever to drink them.

Eric told me also that once you ordered a drink from the bartender, he would always know what it was. All you had to do was ask for the usual. I was drinking Glenfiddich and the next time I came in I said, "The usual." Amazingly, he produced a shot of Glenfiddich neat. I was impressed.

We began color correcting and making our air tape. As we went along and Larry, Eric, and I asked for things, I felt the color was getting very far from reality. Finally I said, "Pull out all the color corrections." The colorist did. "Fine," I said. "Now just balance the individual shots." We were going too far with the technology and making the movie look like a Disney cartoon.

We returned to Cinecitta, and Maureen and I finished preparing the two-parter for the Italians. Most of the crew was gone by this time, and we were alone. While I was mixing this version, Maureen went around Italy touring. When I finished, Eric asked me to take the negative back to Los Angeles with me.

"I'm not going home," I said.

"What?" he asked.

"I have nothing to rush home to. I think I'll explore Europe. I'll head east, maybe see Germany."

I cashed in my first class ticket and took the money. I took a train to Bari and crossed the sea to Dubrovnik. The sun was coming up as we sailed in to that beautiful walled town. I spent a day there and took the night plane to Belgrade. I was lonesome, so I caught a plane to Paris and linked up with Gabrielle Tana from the crew.

She found me a cheap ticket to New York. I had to go to Luxemburg to catch the plane and it flew me to Reykjavik, Iceland, before depositing me in New York. I stayed with friends on the East Coast before taking a cheap flight via Chicago to Los Angeles. It took me about three months to get home. It was just in time to catch *The Fifth Missile* on NBC.

Chapter 24

Dede Allen: The Best There Was and Ever Will Be

Aunt Dede, as I used to call her, was the best there was and ever will be. Nobody was in her league. Starting with *Odds Against Tomorrow* and *The Hustler*, she would go on to edit such classics as *Bonnie and Clyde*, *Little Big Man*, and *Reds*. Her first cuts were so complete, they could have been theater releases.

Dede's first cut of *Let It Ride* was perfect. The studio then spent six months trying to make it better—to no avail. The sound editors began calling the show "Let It Die." Eventually, it was considered finished and went on to whatever its film destiny was, but to its credit, the best hands in editing had been on it.

I first met Dorothea Corothers Allen at a dinner party at my house in the late

Figure 24.1. Dede Allen.

1980s. I had just returned from working with producer Eric Bercovici on the NBC movie of the week, *The Fifth Missile*, which we had made in Italy at Cinecittà Studios in Rome. Dede, as she was called, was Eric Bercovici's aunt by marriage. She was accompanied by her husband of many years, Steven, and Eric was accompanied by my coeditor of the film, Maureen O'Connell.

From that moment on, we became friends, and Dede and I met from time to time, usually in social situations. She was a warm, generous person who frequently spoke to classes I was teaching and even allowed many of my students to interview her. Over the years, I learned much about her through our conversations.

Dede started out as an assistant editor at Columbia Pictures in Hollywood in the 1940s. At that time, for a woman to move up to full editor wasn't that easy. Eventually, Dede and Steven moved to New York, I believe because of Steven's work. There, she began editing commercials and started to make a name for herself.

Dede had a great sense of drama and pacing. Perhaps she inherited it from her mother, who had been an actress. At an early age, she was exposed to artistic people who had an influence on her. She had perfect instincts as to where to cut at any given time and how long to hold the cut.

Despite rumors to the contrary, Dede's career began rather modestly with a little feature in 1948 called *Because of Eve*. She did not cut another feature until the year 1958, when she did *Terror from the Year 5000*, a somewhat forgettable sci-fi film. Her next film was an "A" picture for Robert Wise, *The Odds Against Tomorrow*.

I asked Dede, "How does one go from *Terror from the Year 5000* to *The Odds Against Tomorrow*?" She simply replied, "Robert Wise hired me." The simplicity of her answer left me speechless. Indeed, Robert Wise did hire her. He came to New York to make the picture and found that the editor he wanted to hire was already on a project. That editor recommended Dede Allen. Wise met with her and hired her.

Dede was worried about working for such a noted director. She tried various approaches to each scene. When at last she ran a cut scene for Wise, he noticed the many splices as the film ran through the projector. "This is great," he said. "You've tried several ways to cut the scene." From that moment on, Dede was home free. Wise knew he had the right editor.

A few pictures later, she was doing Robert Rossen's *The Hustler*, the evocative, smoky drama that put poolrooms on the map and made Paul Newman an authentic movie star. Dede Allen was now an "A" list editor, though a New York one at that. In those days, the East Coast Editors Guild and the West Coast Editors Guild were separate unions. Dede belonged to the East Coast guild and therefore was not eligible for West Coast pictures. Eventually, she was allowed to join the West Coast union, and subsequently the two merged as a national union.

With *Bonnie and Clyde*, Dede began her long-term relationship with producer-actor Warren Beatty. The film has a raw energy inherent in the cuts that move the story along to a violent cinematic conclusion that is iconic and which changed the rules of filmmaking.

Dede Allen was the much-sought-after queen of picture cutters. At Paramount, she collaborated with Cecelia Hall, the queen of sound editors. They were an awesome pair, doing *Let it Ride* and *The Addams Family*. At times, she would encounter youthful studio executives who would mouth such things as, "I'm worried we don't have over-the-shoulder shots." Dede would reply, "You should only be worried if I'm worried."

Sometimes, she would end the conversation by looking over the top of her glasses and asking the youthful exec, "How old are you?" That would usually end the discussion.

Dede's editing was always spot-on and drove the story dramatically. She worked for such directors as Paul Newman, Arthur Penn, and Warren Beatty when he directed his epic *Reds*. When she received the ACE Lifetime Achievement Award, Beatty was there. He gave her eulogy at Warner Bros. Studios when she passed away in 2010.

It was my privilege to know her.

Credits

Fig. 24.1: Image of Dede Allen by American Cinema Editors. Copyright © by Estate of Dede Allen. Reprinted with permission.

Chapter 25

John Travers: An Editor for All Seasons

O
n a rainy Sunday in January, an exclusive group of friends and associates gathered at the historic Egyptian Theater where John Travers had spent so much time to pay a last goodbye to a little known, but incredibly talented, film editor. The theatre gave us the Spielberg room in honor of him. He passed away alone of a heart attack in his bungalow at Yamashiro Restaurant in the Hollywood Hills on November 1, 2017. He had been working hard editing on a schedule that was unrealistic and demanding, but that was like John.

John Travers was an editor for all seasons. He was of the faith, and lived and breathed film. To many of the young filmmakers who came to Hollywood, he was their inspiration. I was privileged to work with him on two films, *One Down* and *Lightmaker*. On *One Down*, we began working on the film in his tiny bungalow at Yamashiro. It was a recut, and we were working with a limited budget. Eventually, I secured a room for us at Warner Hollywood Studios.

John was a constant source of inspiration on how to make the movie better. I don't remember much about the film, but I do remember John having me, my brother, Thom; and several other people come to a cemetery as mourners for a key scene he wanted to add. He was having trouble shooting with a Russian camera he had acquired. The camera wouldn't work and we never got the scene, but nobody minded being there for John.

Later as we were reshaping the film, we had a scheduled screening and John was

Figure 25.1. John Travers.

still wrestling with reel three. I grabbed the other reels and headed for the screening room on the lot yelling back to John, "You have fifteen minutes to finish the reel before we hit white screen!" Fourteen minutes later John walked into the screening room, and shortly thereafter reel three came up. It played beautifully. Under that pressure, John did what he always did. He made the picture better.

I don't remember how I met John Travers; probably through Doug Haines or Bob Murawski, ACE. I later learned he was born in New Orleans and grew up in Connecticut. His father was the novelist Robert Travers, and his half sister was Mary Travers of the folk group Peter, Paul, and Mary. None of this did he ever tell me. I only found this out after his passing.

He became a filmmaker at age eleven, making his own films. While in high school he worked as a production assistant on *Friday the 13th* for director Sean Cunningham and producer Steve Miner. While at the University of Bridgeport he won the ACE Student Eddie in 1981. He topped this in 1986 when he won the Student Academy Award for his forty-four-minute film *Jenny*. I had never seen the film until the memorial and was astounded by the work and craftsmanship that went into it. His ongoing love affair with editing began with that film.

After working together, I would often run into John, usually at the Egyptian where he filmed events, including Invisible Art/Visible Artists. He would usually take me next door and buy me dinner, and we would talk film. He had strong insight into how editing made the movie.

At one point, John showed me the feature he had directed, *Deep Down*, with George Segal and Tanya Roberts. I wondered why he didn't direct more, but I guess his real love was editing. Among other films he edited are the documentary *Peter, Paul and Mary:*

Figure 25.2a. The memorial service at the Egyptian.

Figure 25.2b. The memorial service at the Egyptian.

Reunion, *Meeting Spencer*, and *Convincing Clooney*, as well as several television series, including *Hollywood Safari* and *Billionaires Car Club*. He also edited trailers, music videos, and commercials.

A few years later we collaborated on *Lightmaker*, a film that had gone through many versions. John brought me on to help organize the footage from the many versions. It was a huge task, and as I managed it I was able to watch John at work. His innate sense of story and creativity allowed him to bring out elements not previously explored and often he shot new footage to make the story work.

At the memorial service, we viewed *Jenny*, and many of his friends and associates told stories of his love of film, his compassion for his friends, and his fondness for getting together at the historic Formosa across from the old Samuel Goldwyn lot. I will always regret that I never asked John to join ACE. He very much exemplified the editors ACE is looking for: devoted to the craft.

Chapter 26   *How to Get a Job*

After leaving the Air Force back in 1968, I didn't know a soul when I came to Hollywood. I had no connections in the industry. I had learned my craft in the service and had no ties with Hollywood. Fortunately, I was unmarried and under no obligations. So, at the end of my enlistment, I hitched a ride and came to Hollywood.

Someone had given me the name of a small production house, Filmline Production Associates; I had no other contacts. I applied at Filmline, but they had just hired someone. Through an employment agency, I got a job as an office boy at Price Waterhouse, the accounting firm that counts the ballots for the Academy Awards. Two weeks later, Filmline called me and said the other person was not working out and asked if I would like the job. Thus began five decades of moving from job to job and film to film, only rarely having a steady job.

Writers write, directors direct, and editors edit. Even if you are working for free, editing for a friend, you are editing. Every job is an opportunity to learn, to make new contacts, and demonstrate your abilities. Eventually, you'll find someone who will pay you. (You will never get a job from the Department of Employment.) People will hire you because you have been recommended by someone they trust.

My time at Paramount came about because of George Watters, who was running television postproduction. I had met him when he was cutting a picture down the hall from my cutting room. We had coffee together and talked. When an opportunity arose, he brought me to Paramount. When I arrived there, I already had 17 years' experience working on low-budget films, so I was ready for the project.

Today, there are many opportunities to make connections for editing. Learning to edit is one of the best reasons for attending film school. You can learn all you need to know about filmmaking on the set and in cutting rooms, but film school can give you connections. These connections are valuable because these are the future filmmakers. Many a young director has found his editor among fellow students.

When I was cutting a lot of low-budget films where I couldn't afford a first-class assistant, I would train my own. I would find a second assistant who wanted to be a first, and I would hire them. In return for working at a low rate, I would show them all the secrets I had learned over the years in editing. Many of these assistants have since gone on to successful editing careers.

The trick to getting a job is being there. It's one thing to send out a lot of résumés, but that is just paper or e-mail. It's best to try to go to companies and hand deliver résumés. This is not always easy to do, but the advantage is that potential employers have a chance to see you and form an opinion. It personalizes you.

To keep my hand in things, I go to a lot of editing functions just to be seen so people will not forget me. For someone wanting to pursue a career in editing, this is invaluable. If you're not in Los Angeles or New York, it may not be so easy to find people making films. But with the computer technology we now have, filmmakers are everywhere—so wherever you are, there are opportunities. You have to look for them and not give up. Only you can make your future.

Chapter 27 *Working in Sound*

When sound was added to film beginning with *The Jazz Singer*, it was merely for the purpose of dialog. Quickly it was seen that music could strongly affect the screen images and greatly enhance the story. This is why silent films had an orchestral accompaniment, either live or on records. Sound effects, it was learned, could also do much to the emotional impact of the story. Sound in a movie is not intended to be reality.

Sound is an artistic tool of storytelling. It is not so much what a scene sounds like as what dramatically it should sound like to fit the story. In Chapter 10, I described how sound effects overpower dialog when Terry confesses to Edie in *On the Waterfront*. It adds an intensity to the scene. I have no idea how it really sounded when they shot the scene, and I don't care. The important thing is how the sound enhances the storytelling.

The great sound editors like Mike LeMaire, Richard Anderson, George Waters II, Steve Flick, and Cecelia Hall have a vision of the sound in their head, just like Wolfgang Amadeus Mozart did as he composed music. And like the composer, they create a sound track that tells the story. When Martin Scorsese was making *Raging Bull*, his sound editor Frank Warner asked him, "Who's going to score the picture?" The director replied, "You are." It was true, as aside from some classical music there is no other score than the sound effects that carry the film.

With the advent of the digital revolution, sound has not been neglected. When we were on film building dialog, effects, ADR, foley, and music tracks, the work was very labor intense and required actually building reels of each track. Between the various sounds, we ran fill leader to keep the elements in sync. Fill leader is old release prints that have been taken out of circulation. When I first started *Shogun* at Paramount, I thought I was hot stuff. Then I looked down at my fill leader and realized it was a reel from *The Godfather*. At that point, I realized the final end of film production was fill leader. All our artistic efforts would eventually end up as fill leader on someone else's show.

That was disillusioning, but I eventually got over it. The fill leader spliced in between the sound elements physically maintained the sync. It was spliced in base up so emulsion would not build up on the heads as it played on the dummy machines during the mix. It took many tracks to create the sounds for each reel. I remember when Cecelia Hall was doing the sound on *Star Trek: The Motion Picture*, she built 200 separate tracks for Reel One. Just moving the tracks to the stage was a major job.

Now we do it all digitally in a computer and just show up with drives. Physically it's much easier, but it still is the same job. You are building tracks in the computer, not on the bench, and you no longer need fill leader. You park the sounds where they belong based on time code. I was fortunate to get to work in sound when we were still on film and learn some of the tricks of the trade.

I rate sound editors by how they cut dialog. That's what drives the story forward: the words between the actors. When I worked for Eric Bercovici at MGM he told me in regards to mixing his shows. "I don't care about foley. I don't care about sound effects. I don't care about music. I only care about the dialog. I wrote it. I want to hear it." In some ways, Eric was right. The dialog is the main sound that needs to lead the other sounds.

Dialog editing is much like color correction. You want it all to be balanced and seem to be happening as you watch the film. Whatever direction a mike is pointed in, the sound will be different when you switch angles. In dialog editing you separate your tracks and overlap them so the dialog mixer can blend them together to make them sound the same. Sometimes words need to be altered or finessed to make their meaning clear.

Eventually you end with a dialog premix that has all the dialog placed and balanced to work with the other tracks. When ADR is used, the background for the original line must be filled with that background so the new line is indistinguishable from the other lines that have not been replaced. Then you have effects and foley to deal with.

Effects can be almost anything from gunshots to tire squeals. Some of these sounds may actually be on the production track, but they probably need to be replaced or at least added to. The advantage of having these on separate tracks is that in the mix you can decide at what level each sound should play.

Foley, as already described in Chapter 8, is the synchronous recording of sound effects to picture. It is footsteps, body movements, props, et cetera—all shot to the picture on the screen. Some of this overlaps with sound effects. When I edited the foley on reel one of *The Godfather III*, I had thirty-six separate tracks of which eighteen were footsteps. Every character in the opening scene in the church had a separate track of footsteps. Then there were eighteen tracks of props that actually included the wind in the trees, water laps, and any and all props being used.

In 35 mm, we had to sync these sounds up to the quarter frame. It is recorded as close to sync as the foley person can make it, but it does require a little slipping and sliding to line up exactly. The precision has to be exact. Sound work gives editors a discipline you don't find in picture. The work required a precision that many picture editors are not capable of.

Foley serves two important purposes. One, it allows the filmmaker to raise and lower sounds for dramatic purpose. Two, on a foreign mix it fills in when the production track dialog is gone. For a foreign language version, when you drop the production dialog, it leaves a huge hole in the sound. Here is where foley fills in and when the foreign voices are added. The film plays just like the domestic version.

The foley and effects tracks are then premixed for the final. With these premixes, the music can then be added in and a final mix with everything can happen. After checking, a print master can be made through Dolby for release printing. A print master essentially combines all the tracks together which when played back through the proper decoder spreads the tracks to the proper speakers.

When I first started out, many films were simply mono, leaving you with a master dialog, a master effects, and a master music. Three elements combined together, they became your mono master track that was laid down on a release print to play back through a projector. Pulling the dialog master left you with a master music and a master effects track that was known as your M&E (music and effects master) or international track. Before shipping foreign, a mix had to be done adding foley to fill in where production dialog had been removed. The foreign customer had only to add in their dialog to achieve a proper track for their market.

As described in Chapter 17, sound is advanced twenty frames on release prints. This made combining reels problematic. Theaters stopped using two projectors, and films were made up on platers so the film could be run without a projectionist. To make this flawless in the mix, we made pullups. The first twenty frames of reel 2 would be duplicated and attached to the end of reel 1. The first twenty frames of reel 3 would be attached to the end of reel 2 and so on. In this way, with the sound advanced and all the reels spliced together, no sound was lost.

Stereophonic sound made it a little more complicated. Starting in 1953 with Cinerama and the Cinemascope epics like *The Robe*, studios started making films with stereophonic sound to compete with television. Stereophonic sound had been used in Disney's *Fantasia* back in 1939, but other than that, films had been mono. Cinerama's *This Is Cinerama* featured seven-track stereophonic sound to further enhance the excitement of their process.

With Cinerama, however, the sound was played on a separate machine synchronized to the three projectors showing the film. If you will refer to the Cinerama illustration in Chapter 15, you can see there were four speakers behind the screen and three in the back of the theater. The sound player played back seven separate tracks, each track assigned to a specific speaker.

Initially, studio films had merely left and right sound with a phantom center that only required two tracks on the print. When larger formats started coming into use, such as 55 mm and 70 mm, it was possible to add more tracks. Seventy-millimeter print is 65 mm picture with 5 mm for the sound track. The best stereo I ever heard was in *Cleopatra* where the actor's dialog actually came from a speaker positioned behind the screen near where the character was. This was great sound but rather difficult for mass marketing a film.

A matrix was needed to take all the tracks for various speakers, combine them to two tracks on the print, and then play them back to the proper speakers when ran through a decoder. Dolby does this quite well, and they were able to beat out their competitors in marketing their print master matrix. When surround sound came along with films like *Earthquake*, it was easy enough to work these speakers into the Dolby matrix. So now you end up with not one master, but seven masters that each have dialog, effects, and music balanced on them that go together to make the print master for the release print.

In the early days, picture editors did their own sound editing, but very quickly it became something specialized. The individual aspects of sound dialog, ADR, effects, foley, and music are all specialized. Usually there is a supervising sound editor who is responsible for the whole sound editing package. That person hires editors to handle each of these aspects and is on the stage for the mix to make sure it all worked as it should.

Among the best of them is Cecelia Hall, who was nominated for sound editing on *Top Gun* and *The Hunt for Red October*. On both of these films, she recorded much of the sound effects, supervised their editing, and literally directed the mix. She had a vision of how it should sound, and she directed everyone to that vision. On *Top Gun*, she drove the mixers mercilessly, but they walked away with Oscars, as she did on *The Hunt for Red October*.

Ben Burtt, who has done many of the Skywalker projects, decided to elevate the position of sound editor by taking a credit as sound designer. He became alarmed when the Academy informed him that sound designer was not a category they gave an award for. Somehow, he managed to straighten them out, and you now see several people using this credit. Sound designer used to refer to someone creating a special sound effect. Now it's for the person responsible for supervising the whole sound package.

Regardless of what they are called, there needs to be people of auditory vision guiding the film through sound editing and the mix. Otherwise, all the fine work of cast and crew is wasted at the finishing line.

Chapter 28

The Influence of the French New Wave

Television, as I have described, had a big influence on editing. The traditional methods of telling stories were changing. In France new filmmakers were breaking the so-called rules of editing. They were christened the "New Wave." Jump cuts were allowed. A new artistic expression was in the air. With the increasing interest in world cinema, all of this was destined to come back to Hollywood.

It all came home with *The Pawnbroker* in 1964. It was a little New York film, but its influence was huge. The story concerns Sol Nazerman (Rod Steiger), a Jewish pawnbroker in Harlem. He is a survivor of the Holocaust, but his wife and children were murdered in a concentration camp. He lives, but he is dead inside. He eats, sleeps, screws, and goes to work, but these are all empty acts. He is dead, and he cares for no one. The story is of his regeneration by caring for another human being.

To tell this story, the audience needs the backstory. In *Casablanca*, the backstory of Rick's (Humphrey Bogart's) romance with Ilsa (Ingrid Bergman) is also important. We learn about it when Ilsa and her husband, Victor Laslo (Paul Henreid), walk into Rick's Café. Later, Rick sits in the dark listening to Dooley Wilson play "As Time Goes By." The camera moves in on Rick. There is a soft dissolve to Rick and Ilsa driving through Paris, and we're into the flashback. It works well.

It would not work this way for *The Pawnbroker*. The backstory is too grim. Editor Ralph Rosenbloom and director Sidney Lumet went into their backstory with flash cuts. As Sol locks up and leaves his shop, he stares at the calendar date of September 29. It has some significance to him. Then, as he walks to his car, we hear the sounds of dogs barking. There is a flash cut of a German soldier running with a German Shepherd It's only six frames, but you recognize the image. It happens again. Then there is a flash cut of a concentration camp inmate running and trying to climb a fence. Back in the present, some boys are beating another boy inside a fence.

Figure 28.1. Traditional flashback. 1. Rick cries in his beer; 2. Dissolve to Paris; and 3. Rick and Ilsa driving in CASABLANCA (1942), Warner Bros.

Sol watches, and we move into the flashback of Sol, as an inmate, watching the other man trying to escape as the German Shepherd grabs his leg and pulls him from the fence. Sol can only watch in horror. We cut back to the present, and Sol is visibly shaken. This little sequence changed editing in America.

The idea for the flash cut had been taken from the French film *Hiroshima, Mon Amour*. It was used sparingly in that film, but it left an impression. With its use in *The Pawnbroker*, the editing rules began to crumble.

Other films began using the flash cut. It could cue a memory, and it also could show what a character was thinking. A man could be looking at a woman, and then there would be a flash cut of them making love. It would be obvious what he is thinking. We now had a new tool for exploring inner character.

In 1965 Ralph Rosenbaum edited a film called *A Thousand Clowns*. It was from a Broadway play, and the majority of the story takes place in a small apartment belonging to Murray, the main character. Fred Coe directed it and promptly went back to the Broadway stage, his main element. The film resembled what it was: a stage play. Herb Gardner, the play's author, was not satisfied with this. He wanted something more cinematic.

Figure 28.2. Entering a flashback through flash cuts in THE PAWNBROKER (1964), Paramount Pictures.

Gardner started by bringing in music of marches. The music was transferred to mag, and Ralph cut stock shots to it. They tried inserting it into the picture to open it up. The results were exciting. Over the next year, Rosenbaum and Gardner began shooting montages to open up the picture even more. Stars Jason Robards and Barbara Harris

Figure 28.3. Bicycle montage in A THOUSAND CLOWNS (1965), MGM/UA.

were both New York actors doing plays at the time. On their days off, they could be used in all sorts of montages. They were shot seeing off a ship, in the park, and riding a bicycle built for two. These montages were inserted throughout the picture.

Suddenly, a photographed stage play became something else. Besides opening up the story, it gave the film a very New York feel and added a texture that wasn't there before. In terms of editing, it meant that the only limit is your imagination.

The bicycle montage with "Yes sir That's my baby" playing underneath photographically sold the fact that Robards and Harris were falling in love in a way dialog could not express. It was created in the Editing Room it meant many subtle concepts could be expressed with imaginative editing.

All through the 1960s, new ways of editing were being tried. In *The Thomas Crown Affair* (1968) and *Grand Prix* (1966), split screens were used extensively in telling the story. In *Thomas Crown*, this technique was dramatically used to show the arrival of the bank robbers and the heist itself. In *Grand Prix*, it was used during the racing sequences to add a new dimension and involve the viewer in the 70 mm epic.

Figure 28.4. Split screens used to intensify the race in GRAND PRIX (1966), MGM.

Easy Rider, the movie that changed everything, came along in 1969. Made for under $0.5 million dollars using a crew from the National Association of Broadcast Engineers and Technicians, as opposed to the International Alliance of Theatrical and Stage Employees, the movie became a blockbuster. Produced by a young Peter Fonda, a veteran of nice-guy roles, and directed by Dennis Hopper, who had been blacklisted at the end of the 1950s, it captured the imagination of audiences everywhere. Jack Nicholson, who had worked in obscurity in low-budget Hollywood films, gave a breakout performance.

The film was edited by Donn Cambern, ACE, a former music editor, who had edited only one feature prior to this. I believe that because of his inexperience as a picture editor, he was more open to trying things that a more seasoned editor would have rejected. The transitions were notable in the use of flash cuts to work into a new scene. There would be six frames of the incoming scene, then six of the current scene, then the incoming scene would be shown again. It would happen three times, and then you'd be in the new scene.

In the example below Peter and Dennis are getting stoned. As the scene ends six-Frames of the sun through a broken roof are shown before flashing back to six frames of Peter and Dennis to six more of the sun through the roof and then back again to Peter and Dennis before ending on the sun through the roof and into the morning scene. It was an interesting transition and appropriate to the film, but it did not catch on.

Figure 28.5. Transitions in EASY RIDER (1969), Columbia. Forward, back, forward, back, forward, back, and forward into new scene.

Years later when Danny Cahn and I were editing the pilot for *Out of Time* we used a similar device for shock value where we would use a series of jump cuts to zoom in on something. I used it in *Nightmare on Elm Street IV* when a mother discovers her son drowned in his waterbed. I had a bad zoom so I just jump cut it in. Other editors on the film tried to use it elsewhere as a device, but the waterbed was the only place it really worked.

In the Bordello scene near the end of the movie, Peter Fonda stares at writing on the wall, and there is a flash cut, suggesting his ultimate fate. Screen direction bit the dust on this one. The motorcycles went this way, then that way. The Mardi Gras sequence was shot in 16 mm and had to be blown up to 35 mm for editing. The crosscountry ride was enhanced by hit music from popular groups of the time, such as The Byrds and The Band.

None of these sequences were cut to music. As any narrative editor knows, you cut for the rhythms inherent in the scene. Records were played against sequences and tried. If one worked, it was used, and possibly cuts were adjusted to hit the beat. The film was ninety-five minutes long. Donn Cambern told me that if the film had been longer, it probably would not have worked. At the end of the film, audiences sat stunned. Leo Jaffe, the head of Columbia Pictures, said at first viewing, "I don't know what the fuck this movie means, but I think we're gonna make a fuck of a lot of money with it." And they did.

Easy Rider was the death knell to large studio epics. Suddenly, everyone was scrambling to make the next hip picture. Any filmmaker with long hair and a drug habit could get a meeting at a major studio. None of the films to come after this really matched the success of *Easy Rider*.

That same year, a rock concert in upstate New York was being filmed that would also have an effect on editing. *Woodstock,* which came out in 1970, introduced flatbed editing to Hollywood. The Moviola had been the traditional editing machine for American and British films. It was nonlinear and fast to cut on. In Europe flatbeds were the order of the day. They were linear and had large screens, accommodating several viewers. On a Moviola only one or two people could see.

The German KEM editor could operate with three picture heads and a track head. It could be configured as either 16 mm or 35 mm. This was perfect, because *Woodstock* was shot on 16 mm, and director Michael Wadleigh wanted more than one image on the screen at any one time. Among the editors were Martin Scorsese and Thelma Schoonmaker, ACE.

After *Woodstock* every editor on a major picture had to have a KEM. Because KEM machines were linear, they were too slow for a first cut. The picture would be put together using a Moviola, and then it was prepared for the KEM. Once in first cut, the editor could roll back and forth on the KEM and compare performances with other takes. Two pictures and two soundtracks could run simultaneously. The large picture head made it easy for both director and editor to view.

Figure 28.6. The Steenbeck Flatbed Editing Bench. The bench shown is set for two pictures.

On television shows the KEM often replaced screening rooms for reviewing cuts with the director. Film could be run at higher speeds, making it easier to hunt through footage for something. The KEM was joined by the Steenbeck, and even Moviola manufactured an editing table of its own for a while.

The basic rule remained the same. First cuts were done on the Moviola for speed. For the director's cut, the flatbeds were used because of the size of the picture and the ability to run two pictures and two tracks.

Chapter 29

Real versus Staged

A s I have previously stated, editing is the one thing that makes movies an art form. Without it, you are merely recording something, real or staged. The first movies were real events being recorded, but it didn't take long for filmmakers to begin staging shots.

In 1903, Edwin S. Porter made his masterpiece, *The Great Train Robbery*. The same year he made *The Life of an American Fireman*. As previously stated, this film combined staged footage with real footage. Porter shot film of a volunteer fire brigade rushing to a fire and putting it out. To create excitement, he shot footage of a woman trapped by the fire. That part was staged.

Figure 29.1. Combining staged action with real action in THE LIFE OF AN AMERICAN FIREMAN (1903), Edison.

By combining the staged footage of the woman with the real footage of the firemen racing to put out the fire, excitement was created. Would the firemen arrive in time to rescue the woman and put out the fire? They did, and the audience achieved emotional satisfaction. This was not Porter's first attempt at combining real and staged events.

In 1901, President William McKinley was scheduled to appear at the Pan-American Exhibition in upstate New York. Porter sent a camera crew to record that piece of history. They arrived and filmed McKinley giving a speech. Afterward McKinley departed the stage and was shot by an anarchist, making Teddy Roosevelt the new president.

Porter realized that he had the last-ever recording of McKinley. The assassin was immediately captured and given a speedy trial. He was to be electrocuted in Auburn State Prison for his crime. Porter asked the warden of the prison for permission to film the execution. There was still such a thing as taste in those days, and the request was refused.

Porter was able to get permission to shoot footage of the prison itself. With that achieved, Porter set out to build a mockup of the electric chair and stage the execution with an actor. This he did and put together a film called *Execution of Czolgosz with Panorama of Auburn Prison*. The combining of real and staged began with that.

There were people who wanted to film the world as it was. They were the documentarians, without whose work our knowledge of the past would be much reduced. When I was in Vietnam, what we were doing was essentially recording history for future documentaries. But even though we were essentially covering real events, we often staged things. To make our footage of bombing runs more interesting, we would sometimes shoot a pilot on the ground, pretending to be flying, to be cut into the bombing run.

I'm sure you've all seen footage of the attack on Pearl Harbor by the Japanese Navy on December 7, 1941. The Japanese did not issue a call sheet for movie people to film the attack. It was a sneak attack. Most of the footage you see was shot days later by John Ford, and he restaged things for the camera. Those ships on Battleship Row burned for weeks.

When we were cutting news clips of the Vietnam War for television, we did what all editors do: we told a story. If we were cutting a clip and needed a shot, we would borrow it from another clip if it worked. Our job is to tell a story and make it interesting, and we take our job seriously. Are we altering history? Perhaps, but history is what people say it is. I have no idea how true it is. I know only what the books say. So, when we enhance the footage we are given, we are manipulating it, but, of course, that is what we editors always do.

In the 1980s, I made a film with Begonia Plaza called *Gernika Lives*. It was a documentary about the firebombing of Gernika by the German Condor Legion during the Spanish Civil War and its aftermath. No one filmed that event. There was no advance warning. Footage does not exist. Nevertheless, we created the event using stock footage from the bombings of other cities during World War II. We needed this to tell our story.

It is normal in movies, particularly World War II films, to cut in stock footage of an event to help tell the story. Battleships firing at each other are hard to re-create, and if there is footage available, why not use it? Haskell Wexler, ASC, took it to a new level when he directed *Medium Cool*. It is a film about a television cameraman in Chicago in 1968, the year of the riots at the Democratic Convention.

When the riots began, Haskell took his leading lady and inserted her into the proceedings. As the National Guard is marching in, Verna Bloom is moving through the streets looking for her son. What is going on around her is real. You can even hear on the track somebody saying, "Look out, Haskell. This is real." This is unique: the actor becomes part of the stock footage.

Figure 29.2. The staged merges with reality. Actress Verna Bloom becomes part of the Chicago Riots in MEDIUM COOL (1969), Paramount Pictures.

Oliver Stone used stock footage extensively in *JFK*. Not only did he use it; he created his own footage and made it look like stock. At times it is hard to tell what is staged and what is real.

The film is brilliant. To create the "counter-myth" of the Kennedy assassination, Stone makes it a detective movie, with district attorney Jim Garrison as the detective trying to discover what happened and who was responsible.

The film opens with newsreel footage of President Eisenhower's farewell address to the nation. Through stock shots and some staged footage, Stone creates for his audience the time and the politics of the period. Some of the stock is restaged footage.

Figure 29.3. The close up of Little Girl is restaged to match the wide shot of the actual event in JFK (1991), Warner Bros.

The tossing out of the prostitute, Rose Cheramie, played by Sally Kirkland, from a car driven by conspirators is obviously staged. It is black and white and fits in with the stock shots. It builds to the arrival of the Kennedys at Love Field, the motorcade to Dealey Plaza, and the killing. The Dealey Plaza sequence is enhanced by restaged footage skillfully intercut with actual footage.

We see Abraham Zapruder filming the event, intercut with some of his film. The little girl skipping along the sidewalk is shown from a second angle, obviously restaged. Editors Joe Hutshing, ACE, and Pietro Scalia, ACE, skillfully interwove real and staged events into a perfect blend. From there the action moves into the film itself by going to Kevin Costner as Garrison hearing the news of the assassination in New Orleans. This recreation cleverly merges the two realties; the real footage and the staged footage almost like Wexler did by putting Verna Bloom into the riot footage.

Throughout the film, theories are discussed and shown, disregarding normal continuities. The quest for answers leads the viewer. It is a marvelous construction and very deserving of the Oscar it received for editing. The trial scene uses staged black-and-white footage to illustrate Garrison's theory of the killing.

It has been suggested that *JFK* is a distorted view of history—that people seeing the film today will think that's exactly what happened. Well, it's a movie. It's not history any more than *Lawrence of Arabia* is history. That film is David Lean's concept of T. E. Lawrence, and *JFK* is Oliver Stone's attempt to suggest that Kennedy was killed by a conspiracy, not a lone assassin. In the end, both films have to stand on their merits as stories told well. The truths we deal with are artistic.

Chapter 30

From Gernika Lives to American Empire: My Life in Documentary Editing

I have worked on only a few documentaries over the years. I did one for HBO called *The Time of Our Lives*. It was the history of *Time* magazine and it was scripted. Mostly I had to find the right images to go with the narration. It was both educational and fun, like having a time machine as I sought out film to cover historical events.

Since the mid-seventies I have been fond of eating at a Mexican restaurant called the Casita Del Campo. It was established by Rudy Del Campo, who had been one of the Sharks in Robert Wise's *West Side Story*. He had invested his money in the restaurant. It was on the Hyperion Pass on my way home to my apartment in Los Feliz. I could get a good meal that was inexpensive.

I met a young waitress there named Begonia Plaza and over the years we became friends. She decided to pursue a career as an actress. She was in the Eddie Murphy and Nick Nolte film *48 Hours* and Clint Eastwood's *Heartbreak Ridge*. She called me after finishing her part with Ally Sheedy in *Maid to Order*. She had been in the Basque Country in northern Spain but was back in town to do ADR on the picture.

"I want you to come back to the Basque Country with me," she said.

"What do you have in mind?"

"I have been shooting a documentary in Gernika, and I need you to help me edit. With the money I got for looping I can fly you over and pay you. Will you come?"

"I'd love to. We just have to be careful how we explain this to my girlfriend. She isn't going to want to hear I'm running off to Spain with a beautiful actress. We have to think of another approach."

Fortunately, my girlfriend knew Begonia. The three of us met for lunch, and my girlfriend was thrilled with the idea of me going off to spend six weeks in the Basque Country. So it was settled. Begonia went on ahead, and I was to join her in two weeks.

I was booked on a night flight to Madrid. Seated next to me were two attractive young women. One was a winner from *The Dating Game*. The other was her chaperone from the show. The young man she had won as a date was sitting in the smoking section of the plane. I talked with the women until they fell asleep, as did I. As we disembarked the next morning in Madrid I said to the young woman's date, "I slept with your date last night. Now it's up to you to take care of her for the rest of the date."

In Madrid I changed planes for the short flight to Bilbao, where I was met by Begonia. We drove to Galdakano, where we were staying. She had arranged an apartment owned by K2000 where we could live, and we were provided with a car. I freshened up, and we had dinner in a nearby café.

The next morning, we drove up to the K2000 studio where we would work. It was a modern, recently built studio for both television and movies. One of the main things they did was revoice American movies into the Basque language. Begonia brought me up to date on what we were doing.

The Basques were the original settlers on the Iberian Peninsula. Where they came from, nobody knows. Their country, named Euskadi, is made up of seven provinces. Four are in Spain and three are in France. They are a country within a country, actually two countries. They have no relationship to the Spanish or the French. Their language is not derived from Latin, as are Spanish and French.

In Spain, they were exempt from some laws and had a near autonomous situation. Gernika was their capitol and outside their meeting house stood a tree where for years whenever a Basque left the country he took a piece of bark from the tree with him. In the 1930s, a coalition government made up of several political parties, including the Communists, ruled Spain, and they are said to have granted the Basques self-rule.

In 1936, the fascist General Franco started a revolt against the legally elected government. He was supported in the north by General Molla. The Spanish Civil War grew quickly. The rest of the world chose to stay out of it with the exception the fascist governments of Germany and Italy, who supported Franco. Only the Soviet Union took the side of the legal Spanish Government. There were also international brigades of volunteers, like the Abraham Lincoln Brigade, that fought against fascism.

In 1937, the German Condor Legion aerial bombed the town of Gernika for their fascist ally Franco. This event united the Basques against Franco and his partner General Molla. Franco was able to overrun the entire country and end the war in 1939. During the struggle, many of the Basques had sent their children away to other countries like Mexico, France, and the Soviet Union. One of these children was Begonia's father, Jesus.

Begonia had shot hours of coverage of herself and her father going around the country together. To make a story of this, we decided that our story would be of Jesus taking his daughter around and explaining what happened and why. This was all shot on video, and we had a basic convergence editing system (tape to tape) to work from.

We wanted to tell the story of how Gernika was bombed and how the people survived under Franco. We had a number of witnesses who had been interviewed.

We also wanted to discuss the culture and how things were today. When Franco died in 1956, things loosened up. Under him the Basques were not allowed to speak their own language; it was outlawed, a death penalty offence. After Franco's death, their language was permitted and taught in Basque schools. Signs were in Basque and Spanish.

Under Franco, the ETA had formed, a secret terrorist group dedicated to Basque independence. They were still trying to separate from Spain despite the fact that restrictions had lessened. Several political parties had formed and most of them wanted Basque independence, one way or another.

Fortunately, I had brought the big board that I used in Italy. We began viewing footage and writing out descriptions on strips for the board. We would put them on the board and then arrange them in various order. In this way, we could figure out our structure before we did any editing.

I had learned the concept of the big board from Scott Conrad when I was his second editor on a movie-of-the-week called *Heart of Steel*. As dailies came, in we would make up strips describing the action and as we cut the scenes we would mount them in order, which would let us know where we were with the movie at any given time.

Once we had the structure worked out, we began cutting. We would usually come in around 10:00 a.m. and work till about 10:00 p.m. Afterward, we would go to a local disco to unwind—Begonia would dance and I would drink single-malt scotch. Then around 2:00 a.m. we would go home to sleep. We could go to the local farmer's markets to buy our food.

We also took trips to explore the area. On one of these trips we drove to Madrid, and in the Prado we saw Pablo Picasso's *Guernica*. It was huge, covering an entire wall. He had painted it in Paris after hearing of the bombing, and it is his outcry against the savagery of that day in the town. The images are overwhelming. During Franco's life, Picasso did not allow *Guernica* to be in Spain. After his death, it came to the Prado for the first time.

Begonia would introduce me to various people, and we would explore the town of Gernika, rebuilt since the bombing. As the film came together, we had many interviews in either Basque or Spanish. We wanted the film to be seen by English-speaking people, so we had to deal with the language problem.

Begonia was fluent in all three languages, so she could explain to me what people were saying, but that wouldn't work for an audience. We could do subtitles but that could get complicated, and lots of people don't want to read subtitles. We decided to put together a group of English-speaking people to speak over the original speakers. We would dial down the Spanish or Basque and go with the English overdub.

We got the word out and met with a group of speakers, who we hired. We recorded them at K2000. One of the interviews was with a rock lifter, and Begonia felt I was right for the part. This is a sport similar to weight lifting except it's lifting stones. Begonia directed me and actually with much coaxing got a credible performance out of me.

We had cut the film on a tape-to-tape system, which meant anytime we wanted to make a change we would go another generation down on tape. Fortunately, the system spit out a list so we could do an on-line from the original tapes at maximum resolution. I began doing this with a Basque woman who did the on-line cut. When Begonia wasn't around, we would communicate on cuts with math. Plus two frames, minus six frames and so on. It was difficult, but we made it work.

As we went along we thought of various names for the project, eventually settling on *Gernika Lives*. The point was that Franco and Molla had tried to destroy Gernika and the Basque culture. They were both dead now, and the town was very much alive and flourishing. Begonia's father, Jesus, had written a powerful poem about how Gernika stood "stone upon stone." We used it at the end to sum things up.

My girlfriend phoned me and wanted to know if I was ever coming home. She made it clear I needed to come back. I left Begonia to finish the mix and flew home. A few weeks later she arrived with the film, and I was able to approve the final result.

The next documentary that I became involved with was *James Dean: Forever Young*, directed by my long-time friend Michael Sheridan. Like myself, Sheridan had been inspired by Dean, and after his death he hitchhiked from Pennsylvania to Indiana for the first memorial to the actor's passing. He had met the family and spent fifty years trying to collect copies of Dean's television performances. He had written a script with his brother, Kevin, and spent ten years convincing Warner Bros. that they needed to make this documentary.

Michael brought me on as his co-supervising editor. I only cut one scene. Patrea Patrick ended up doing the editing. I mostly solved problems of dealing with the various formats we had and getting them into the AVID.

After that, Patrea Patrick and I decided we wanted to make a documentary of our own. We had both been aware that America was "going to hell in a handbasket." Processed food was causing diseases, which created customers for the pharmaceutical industry; big business and government were conspiring together; and the banks were out of control, and people were getting squeezed. We thought there might be a single cause for all of this.

We literally did this on our own dime. We had no sponsor. Patrea had a list of people she wanted to interview. She set up interviews, and I figured out how to get to them and film them. Patrea had an HDV camera, and I borrowed a second one. With a set of lights and a sound recorder, we traveled around the country recording people.

Patrea was able to line up such luminaries as Vandana Shiva, G. Edward Griffin, Maude Barlow, John Perkins, Gerald Celente, Jeffrey Smith, John Robbins, Francis Moore Lappe, and David Korten. She would direct and run the A camera. I would run B and sound, do the lights, and shoot stills. Sometimes we would be assisted by Layne Hurley, a former student of mine.

In New York City, we interviewed Tariq Ali, whom both John Lennon ("Power to the People") and the Rolling Stones ("Street Fighting Man") had written songs about. He inspired us to use the name *American Empire* for the film. It best described the chaos of what is going on, "an act of collective madness." The uncritical devotion to capitalism is driving us to destruction. Everything, including people, is being made into a commodity. Everything on the planet is being commodified with no thought to the future.

Patrea edited the film together. She would run versions, and I would give input. Eventually, we had a final version. It ran in theaters in New York and Los Angeles for Academy consideration. We attended many screenings and participated in Q&A sessions. I learned a lot working on the film and was privileged to meet some truly extraordinary people.

Documentaries are the purest form of editing. More than any other genre, the film is made in the cutting room. When we were shooting, we were gathering information, but it was in the cutting room where relationships became apparent, and we were able to find the movie hidden in the footage.

Chapter 31

The Right Stuff and the Manipulation of Time and Space

T
homas Wolfe's best-selling book was a natural for the movies, but there were inherent structural problems. *The Right Stuff* is Wolfe's account of America's entry into the space age with the original seven Mercury astronauts. The "right stuff" refers to a special sort of quality that these men had. The man who truly defined that quality was Chuck Yaeger, who in 1947 broke the sound barrier in the X-1 rocket while suffering from broken ribs. Yaeger never became an astronaut. Without him there was no "right stuff."

Writer/director Phillip Kaufman solved the problem by beginning the movie with Yeager's breaking of the sound barrier, demonstrating that he has the "right stuff." Then we are introduced to Gordon Cooper who, like Yaeger, is a test pilot but is soon destined to become an astronaut. As the story progresses, we meet all of the original seven.

The canvas of the film is huge, incorporating the politics and events of the time. Some of the characters are symbolic, like Royal Dano appearing as a preacher symbolizing death. The government men portrayed by Jeff Goldblum and Harry Shearer are almost comic book characters as they stumble around trying to find America's best pilots. They aren't interested in Yaeger because he is not a college graduate. The portrayals of Eisenhower and Johnson are broad.

The film is not a history of what happened but rather a look at what the events meant. Also, it captures the paranoia of the time when the Soviets beat America by putting the satellite Sputnik into orbit. Then they had the first man in space, Yuri Gagarin. America was desperate to catch up and not lose face. Much of this was a "dog and pony" show to prove that American capitalists are better than Soviet communists. Everything the astronauts did was treated as a big deal. Even when Gus Grissom panicked and lost his capsule, it was considered a resounding success. Occasionally the film cuts back to Yaeger to keep him alive.

The film climaxes with a large party thrown at the Houston Astrodome by President Johnson for the Mercury astronauts. They are wined and dined, while on stage the famous fan dancer Sally Rand performs her dance. This is intercut with Chuck Yaeger test piloting the F-102 back at Edwards Air Force Base. He takes the plane to 102,000 feet where he is beyond the atmosphere and can see the stars before the jet flames out and he is forced to bail out and return to Earth.

The purpose of the scene is to contrast Yaeger, who had the "right stuff," with the Mercury astronauts who, although they are brave test pilots, are being used as manufactured heroes for their government, putting on a show much like Sally Rand is doing with her fans. They were shot into space in capsules over which they had little control, while Yaeger flew into space on his own, demonstrating the "right stuff." This is the point of the movie.

The ending is manufactured. The party at the Astrodome took place in 1962. Yaeger flew the F-102 into space in 1952, a full ten years earlier. To make the point of the movie, both events are cut to appear to be happening simultaneously. It's not the way it really happened, but in light of the story, it makes the necessary point who really had the "right stuff." It is the proper manipulation of time and space.

The movie answers to a creative truth that is a much higher calling than an actual historic truth.

Chapter 32   *Liquid Editing*

O rson Welles, when told about digital editing, referred to it as "liquid
editing." He was right. It's like writing on water. In digital editing, there
is no cut footage. There is only a list of how you would cut the picture
if indeed you were cutting the picture. This was a hard concept for me
to understand.

Having worked on film, I was used to cutting a piece of film and connecting it to
another piece of film. These pieces I would build onto a reel, which along with other
reels would make up the cut film. It would usually be stored in a film rack when not
being worked on. So, when I cut my first film on a digital system, the EMC2, *Sherlock:
Undercover Dog*, I wanted to know where my cut footage was.

It took me a long time to realize that the cutting that I was doing consisted of simply
making a list of how and when to show portions on the digitized audio and video.
There really was no physical cut that existed. That didn't happen until somebody actually
assembled the negative or went out to a tape. Then a physical cut actually existed.

This makes your cut very vulnerable. It's why you need to back up this data in some
fashion. We used to do this on floppy discs, then CDs or DVDs, but now one of the
little memory sticks that you can carry in your pocket works as well. Then, if something
happens to the cut, you can reinstall it from the little drive.

When Patrea Patrick and I were editing *Shannon's Rainbow* on opposite sides of Olive
Avenue in Burbank, we would email each other the cut list from the reels we were working on. We both had the exact same media on the systems we were using. So did our
assistant, Stacey Astenius. Then it was simply a matter of relinking the cut to the footage,
and each of us could see what the other was doing without actually getting together.

This also meant that all three of us could work simultaneously. Stacey could look
for shots for us while we kept editing ahead. It was like the old days on film, when the
editor and the assistant each had their own Moviola and could work simultaneously.

When we first entered the digital age, Avid machines were incredibly expensive. On a low-budget film you could not necessarily afford to have two of them. This created a breakdown in the relationship between the editor and the assistant. They could not be working side by side.

On my first Avid film, *To the Ends of Time*, I would work during the day until about 6:00 p.m. My assistant, Laurent Johnson, would arrive at about 5:00 p.m., and we would have an hour to discuss our work. Then, at 6:00 p.m., I would leave, and she would begin the daily task of loading dailies and managing the database. Because we had to share the same machine, we were forced to work different hours and rarely saw much of each other. She would leave me notes as to her progress, and then we would briefly see each other again at 5:00 p.m. the next day.

This was a total breakdown in the whole editing mentorship that goes on in the editing room. An assistant editor is an editor in training. By actually working with an editor, an assistant acquires the knowledge and skills that will allow him or her to go out and edit films themselves. Many of today's best editors got their start working under the likes of Michael Kahn, Tom Rolf, Dede Allen, Anne Coates, and Donn Cambern. As I have often said, simply being around such talented editors allows you to pick up skills. It's like a social disease. It's spread by contact.

Avid machines used to sell new for $100,000. When I ran post at PM Entertainment, I used to buy them used for $35,000 to $40,000. When Final Cut Pro came on the market, because of the threat it posed, Avid was forced to rethink its marketing and began coming out with software-based versions at a much lower price. Previously, you bought a system that was both software- and hardware-based. Finally, the company made the Avid Film Composer a software-based system. The student version now sells for $295 and it is virtually the same as the version anyone can buy for $999.

Because of this, an assistant could have his own version of the software on a laptop and could be given the same media as the editor. After the editor completed cutting a scene on the main Avid, he could pass the sequence to his assistant on the laptop, and the assistant could go through the scene and clean up the production tracks while the editor moved ahead with new footage.

Assistants could also cut in sound effects, along with anything else the editor needed. This allowed for a more finished look to cuts without wasting the editor's time. It allowed editing rooms and the editor-assistant relationship to return to the way it was with the Moviola.

Also, it was possible for editors to work at home. All they needed to do was pick up the media and return to their homes to work. This was great for single parents with children. They could email cuts to the director for approval. Occasionally, they would come in for a face to face meeting when necessary.

Digital editing began in the late 1980s and early 1990s. Prior to this, video editing had been subject to the constraints of tape. The convergence systems were essentially tape-to-tape machines. You loaded tape dailies onto one machine and recorded the piece you wanted onto another machine. It was very linear. You scrolled back and forth until you found what you wanted and added it to the cut on the other machine.

If you wanted to add or change a cut in a previously edited sequence, you had to relay the sequence and insert the new cut or take the sequence and use it on the clip side and go down another generation of tape. Neither way was very good.

This was no competition to the Moviola, which has always been inherently nonlinear. To add a cut into a film sequence, you simply rolled down on the bench through the synchronizer and opened the cut where you wanted to insert. Then you inserted the new footage, and you were all set. Systems such as the Montage, Ediflex and the Editroid were created to get around this problem.

With the Ediflex, you worked with eight or twelve sets of dailies. As you went through, you created a list of your cuts. You could then play your cut without going out to tape. What would happen was this: the machine would play the first shot from the cut list off of tape number 1. While this was happening, the computer would race through tape number 2, looking for the second cut, and show it as the first cut finished. Then it would race through tape number 3 for the third cut to play after the second. After tape number 12, it would go back to tape number 1. For a time this worked well and the Ediflex had 85% of the television market.

This worked rather well, in that nothing went to tape until you were satisfied with your cut. The Editroid went one better in that its source material was on laser discs and therefore of a higher quality. But these were pretty much Rube Goldberg "bailing-wire" solutions and did not address the basic problem. I believe that the EMC2 did that.

Figure 32.1. Reversing action to make him talk: SHERLOCK: UNDERCOVER DOG (1994), Westwood Films.

Beginning with the EMC2, the idea was to digitize video footage with a computer, where it could be stored, played, and edited. The machine was fairly crude, but it worked. Video footage was captured at low resolution, at 30fps. When playing back, it showed you only fifteen of the thirty frames at any given time. We tended to refer to the image we saw as "pixie vision." Nevertheless, it was possible to edit together a film totally on the computer without going back to tape. That was the system's strength.

I edited *Sherlock: Undercover Dog* on location on the island of Catalina, in the town of Avalon, using the EMC2 system. My assistant was Alan Ravick, who owned the system and instructed me in its use. At first I called cuts, and Alan operated the machine, but within a few days I was able to operate despite being completely computer illiterate.

The system allowed us to do fades and dissolves and even reverse action. That was very important, because the movie was about a talking dog. To simulate conversation, the dog's trainer would put something in the dog's mouth to chew on. While the dog chewed, the director, Richard Gardner, would give the dog's line. Played straight forward, it didn't look that good, but when the action was reversed, it sold the idea that the dog was talking.

When the cut was finished, we created an EDL (edit decision list) that went to a post house, which then created a higher-resolution version of my cut. In those days, drives were not very big, and the offline (creative) editing had to be done at low resolution. The online (conform) editing was done at the post house. The film was shot in 16 mm, but we never went back to the film. It was merely the capture medium.

On the heels of the EMC2, the Avid and Lightworks were developed. They were both 30fps systems, but you could see all of the frames. Lightworks was designed to be editor-friendly. Knowing that most editors had trouble with light switches, the machine was laid out like a flatbed film editing system. It had a joystick to control forward and backward motion, as well as speed.

Most feature film editors went to Lightworks because of these factors. In the early days, it looked like it would be the dominant system. Avid, on the other hand, was very much a computer. You needed to know how to drag and drop, and you controlled the machine with a mouse and the keyboard. These were not things that most of us were familiar with.

The advantage with Avid was that there was a number of opticals or special effects that the system could handle. These advantages eventually overpowered Lightworks, though many editors remained loyal to it.

Avid was a Mac-based system, and Lightworks was PC-based. At some point Apple and Avid had a falling out. Avid decided that it was going to move to PC. This disturbed the many loyal Mac editors, and they protested. Avid decided that it would develop its new software first for the PC and then for Mac. It designed the program to work with either platform.

Apple felt that it needed its own editing system. It purchased a PC-based system and converted it to Mac-only. It was redesigned with many of the same attributes of

Avid, and it was renamed Final Cut Pro. Apple embarked on a campaign of promoting the software, and because of its pricing, it caught on.

Before its demise, Lightworks developed a system of 24fps editing. This was key for editing things shot on film. Because films are shot at 24fps, they are not compatible with 30fps television. As described earlier, films were telecined using the 3:2 pull-downs to become 30fps tapes. Then they could be digitized onto a computer.

If one chose to edit a film on a computer at 30fps, there was no frame accuracy. Because only the "A" frame matches the film "A" frame, we have a problem. Four out of five video frames are mongrels that do not match the film frames. Therefore, if you make a cut anywhere but the "A" frame, it is in doubt where the film cut would be.

Mathematical formulas such as Slingshot were developed to decide where the cut would go, and they worked well enough. But picture editors are picky about the frame they cut on. They don't want the frame changed arbitrarily. If the cut moves a frame, it might be a bad frame. This made cutting a film at 30fps unreliable if you intend to go back to film.

Lightworks dealt with the problem by reversing the 3:2 pull-down when capturing it into the system. This meant that every frame in the computer exactly matched a frame of the negative. This was a great breakthrough for editing features digitally. Film was shot at 24fps, telecined to 30fps (29.98), and digitized into the system at 24fps.

Avid adapted the reversal of 3:2 pull-down to its system. This was what sounded the death knell for the Moviola. Now you could edit on a computer as accurately as on the Moviola. Plus, you had all of the advantages of computer editing. Because of working at 24fps, the Avid could generate an absolutely accurate cut list for the negative cutter.

Gradually throughout the 1990s, the Avid began to take over. Fewer films were being edited on film. The most notable holdout was Stephen Spielberg. He and his editor, Michael Kahn, continued editing on film up until 2010. *Indiana Jones and the Kingdom of the Crystal Skull* was the last major film cut on a Moviola.

It was becoming difficult to edit on film. Single-stripe 35 mm mag was no longer manufactured in the United States. Labs were closing, and it just wasn't easy to work on film. Most producers shot on film and then went into the Avid for editing. Then they would go to a digital intermediate (DI), and output to film or a digital cinema package (DCP).

When Final Cut Pro (FCP) came out, a number of small post houses purchased it to save money. Actually, Showtime decided to use FCP for that reason. Unfortunately, Showtime's product was going back to film, and because FCP was a 30fps system, it was causing the picture editors to have fits. They were in constant conversation with the negative cutters, making sure that there wasn't a bad frame in there.

FCP finally got with the program and realized that it needed a 24fps option. Film Tool was developed for this purpose. After digitizing you could convert your clips to 24. Walter Murch and the Cohen Brothers went to this system. Murch has worked with both Avid and FCP and has discussed the pros and cons of both systems. The Cohens went to FCP only when they had to give up the Moviola.

Final Cut 7 was a good system, and many editors still use it. When the company went to Final Cut 10, it lost a lot of professional business. Major Hollywood studios favor the Avid. There is a reason for this. Avid was designed as a professional system that is part of a workflow. FCP was created more for home use. You can cut on it and post on YouTube. Besides, FCP is manufactured by Apple. It is an Apple product, just like your iPhone, iPad, and so on are. Apple is not in the editing business. Avid is in the editing business. That is what the company does. It also manufactures Pro Tools, which is the standard of the industry as much as Avid is.

Recently, Premiere has come out with a much-updated editing system. It used to be a real pig, requiring you to render every time you turned around. Now it's giving Final Cut a run for its money. Will it replace Avid? I doubt it. Again, Premiere is not in the editing business. Of all three systems, Avid manages data the best, and in professional filmmaking that is so very important. It's an Avid world.

Chapter 33

To the Ends of Time and Learning the AVID

I was dragged kicking and screaming into the twenty-first century. I had great contempt for electronic editing and wanted no part of it. I was out of work and Jackie Freeman had gotten me a job working in a "boiler room" selling medical billing software over the phone to people who really couldn't afford it. It was not a job I liked, but I needed the money.

Purely by accident I ran into a composer I had worked with years earlier who gave me the name of a producer looking for an editor. The producer turned out to be Todd King, who was preparing a project called *To the Ends of Time*. He was co-producer to Ash Shah, and the film was a fantasy taking place in another world where galleons could fly and there were knights and ladies.

Todd showed me a promotional trailer with lots of fancy effects shots, and I became excited about the project. He took me up to a warehouse normally used for a swap meet where the shooting was to take place. In the parking lot there was a life-sized galleon set and inside were many different models. I was introduced to Markus Rothkranz, chief model maker and director of the film.

I told Markus how impressed I was with his models and the upcoming film. He told me, "I like old movies." I erroneously thought that he was referring to films from the forties, like *The Captain from Castille*. He was referring to *Star Wars* as an old film. That was the first misunderstanding to come between Markus and me.

Todd told me that although they were shooting on film, they wanted to have this cut on the AVID. He asked me if I knew the system. I told him I was familiar with Lightworks and the EMC2, and the AVID would not be a problem. They wanted me to pick out one, and they would buy it for the production. I immediately called my former assistant, Heide Scharfe, who had been teaching the program and was using it to edit *Dr. Quinn, Medicine Woman*. She told me what to tell them to order.

I was hired, and I hired Laurent Johnson who actually had some AVID experience to assist me. The AVID was hardware based and it cost about $100,000. It was delivered, and the technicians set it up. When Heidi arrived after work she showed me and Laurent some basics of using the system. For Laurent, it was how to capture from a three-quarter deck, check the database, and arrange shots in scene bins for me to work from.

She showed me how to load clips into the monitor, how to mark an in and out, and how to splice into the time line. After a few days of dailies, Ash Shah came in and wanted me to cut a promo for him. I was able to convince him to wait tell Heidi came by because she could operate the system faster than me. Ash and I called cuts and Heidi operated, and we were able to make the promo.

I named the AVID Emily. I don't remember why I chose that name, but I felt that since the machine was going to be a big part of the movie, it should have a name. After all, my first Moviola had been named Joe.

When the first day's dailies arrived, I dutifully watched them on a big screen television just like we had done on film. It was shot on 35 mm negative and then transferred to tape in telecine. It wasn't the same as film, but since we weren't printing the negative, there was nothing else to do. After the first week, I stopped watching dailies and just viewed from the scene bins.

As I was editing, I often didn't know how to perform certain functions. I would phone Heidi's cutting room, and her assistant would explain what I needed to do. Initially I was calling a lot, but after a couple of weeks the calls became fewer and fewer. Working on the system, I learned what I needed to know to get the job done.

We were shooting for thirty-six days, and this became a problem. Timecode, unfortunately, is based on a 24-hour clock. So, our first day's dailies were Tape VTR 1 with timecode hour 1 (01:00:00:00). This worked fine up through the first twenty-four days. On the twenty-fifth day, the telecine operator called the tape VTR 1 again, timecode 01:00:00:00. The twenty-sixth day became VTR 2, time code 02:00:00:00. When Laurent loaded this into the AVID, it changed the database for the material shot on day one and day two. Suddenly all my cuts began changing. The new timecode was overwriting the old timecode.

We had a meeting with Deluxe, which was providing the telecine. It became clear what the problems was. On the twenty-fifth day, the tape should read VTR 25, timecode 01:00:00:00. The lab tried to blame us for not catching this, but I pointed out that whether we caught it or not, it was still the telecine operator's error. We received new tapes for twenty-five on, and Laurent had to reload the earlier tapes. Deluxe knocked a substantial amount off the bill because of this error.

Because we only had the one AVID, Laurent had to work nights and I worked days. Keith Bewick cut in sound effects for me when he could get on the AVID. The opening of the film was a large assault on a castle by the flying ships.

We also had a problem with Markus, our director. He had his own camera, and he was grabbing shots with it. The script girl had no idea what he was shooting because he would change angles and zoom in or out without warning. It made it very difficult to tell if a scene was properly covered. I made a suggestion to the director of photography. "You're on a concrete floor. If you accidentally knock his camera over, you'll no longer have a problem." Unfortunately, he didn't take the hint.

Markus and I clashed when we had to shoot a pickup shot of some actors entering a scene. Markus wanted them to enter from the right. I insisted they had to enter from the left. We ended up shooting it both ways. We were definitely not getting along.

A few days later I got a call from the script girl. She told me that Markus had refused to shoot a closeup of Joss Ackland, who was playing the king. It was a dialog scene between the king, his daughter, and the hero. They got closeups, the king did not. The script girl had asked for it and so had the assistant director, but Markus had refused.

I saw the footage the next day and wrote up a memo for the set that read something like this: "You will immediately stop shooting and shoot me a closeup of Joss Ackland for last night's scene. THIS IS NOT A REQUEST."

I sent the memo off and shortly thereafter I got a call from Todd King.

"What do you mean, this is not a request," Todd asked? "The director has the right to shoot what he feels he needs."

"Not in this case," I replied. "Joss is the best actor in the scene and in the master, his back is to the camera. You don't have a scene without that closeup."

They shot it and it became known as the Jack Tucker Closeup. It's in the movie. I don't know why Markus didn't want to shoot it.

We had a number of background plates that needed to be in the film through blue screens. These shots were photographed in the old Vista-Vision system to make perfect registration. In this system, the film is five perforations wide and runs through the camera sideways, which makes for a rock steady image.

Markus was very clever in his shooting. He considered the sky to be a big blue screen, and we were able to create shots pulling the blue from the sky to make a composite image.

As we were coming to the end of principal photography, I was energetically getting my cut ready to show. I insisted that we run it in Ash's apartment on his big screen TV. We were an epic, and I didn't want people looking at it on anything small. I laid a temp score, and the screening went well.

Now it was time for Markus and me to work together. He came in and we went through a few scenes where I made his changes. Then we came to a large dialog scene where he had shot some of the coverage. At a certain point, he wanted to go in close and wondered why I had cut the scene the way I had. The close shots were on his camera. We pulled up the shot and went to the spot we were looking for. Unfortunately, Markus had paned away to something else, and we didn't have the shot.

Markus is very smart, and he immediately realized the folly of shooting on his own and not as part of an organized effort. As we continued editing, we both came to respect each other and our respective talents. We had a number of "glass shots" where Markus had painted something over glass and it was placed in front of the camera to create an "in camera" special effect.

We still had a couple of sequences that we had not covered in principal photography. When Markus went to shoot them, he brought me along. He always would ask me which side of the camera the actors should enter from. Half the time it didn't matter, but I would always tell him a side, and he would set up the shot that way.

We finally locked the picture so sound work could begin. I pleaded with Ash Shah to let us mix the picture on a big screen instead of somebody's system in a garage. Eckart Seeber wrote us an epic score, and he recorded it in Eastern Europe where a large orchestra was not that expensive. Patrick Griffith supervised the sound editing, and we did end up mixing on a fairly large stage.

When we viewed the answer print, it all looked good. I did discover, though, the difference between my timing on the AVID and the big screen. There were a few cuts that should have played longer on the screen, but overall it all worked. This was one of the problems with working on a computer where you do not see it on the screen until

Figure 33.1. TO THE ENDS OF TIME, showing a "glass shot" of downed ships.

it's too late. Working on film, we were constantly projecting our work and seeing it in theater conditions. It makes a difference.

A few months later I happened to be in the Crest National film lab when I found out that they were making thirty prints of the film for China. I asked the timer who was advising him on the color. He said no one, so I volunteered to sit in on the timing.

Later, I was hired on a film called *Earth Minus Zero*. It was another AVID show, and I was able to use all that I had learned on my first AVID show.

Chapter 34

The Changing Face of Editing

Technology has completely changed the face of editing. When we worked on film, we basically dealt with editing the picture. Dailies came in and were synced up by the assistant. Track usually arrived at the studio at 6:00 a.m., and the assistants popped the track. They went through and marked the place where you hear the clapper close, identifying it by scene and take. The picture usually arrived around 9:00 a.m., and the lead assistant began building the dailies.

By this time, the building order and usually the script order were already decided, and the tracks had been broken down for easy assembly to the picture. The assistants knew how many rolls of dailies there would be and what shots would be on which roll. It was all figured out based on the script supervisor's paperwork.

Dailies would run at 10:00 a.m. for the studio. If there was too much work, assistants from other shows would be recruited to help, with the understanding that the favor would be returned. The editor would view the dailies in a screening room with the director while his assistant took notes on his preferences. I would usually walk out of dailies having already cut the sequence in my mind. It only remained to do the actual work.

As the film progressed, other sequences would be cut. Eventually, a whole story would emerge and be shaped into the Editor's Cut. A screening would be arranged, and the director and perhaps the producer would watch it with the editor. Then, the Director's Cut would begin.

For the Editor's Cut, there usually would be minimal sound effects or music added. If there was a large silent piece, I might add a tune to show how the sequence would work, but most of the time, it was just the picture and the production track. When the picture was ready for an important screening, a sound editor and music editor would be brought in to handle that. There would then be a temp mix.

We learned over time not to make our picture and sound cuts straight across. If you did that, it telegraphed that there was a cut. If you offset the sound, it would let the picture cut slide by unnoticed, which was our intention. The idea was that you were watching something actually happen; noticing cuts calls attention to the artificiality of it.

Essentially, the movie had to rise or fall on the editing and the actors' performances. There was no music to tell us how to feel. If it played that way, we knew that it would only be better with music and effects. Also, it gave us time to build the presentation, and we saw scenes evolve and become more complete as elements were added.

When I began working on low-budget films, I would cut a separate sound effects and music track on a flatbed with three sound heads. During screenings, I would do a live mix since we couldn't afford an actual temp mix. With the advent of digital editing, this has become the norm. Editors are now expected to cut the picture, lay sound effects and cut in temp music, and do a temp mix.

And that's not all. They are often required to perform color correction and create opticals. If they don't have a shot they need, the editor is expected to pull it from the Internet. I recently sat in on a Director's Cut on a pilot. The director spent all of his time asking for stock shots, sound effects, and music instead of concentrating on the picture editing. He said he couldn't tell if something worked if he didn't see it with music and effects.

This is not the editing world I used to know. Is it wrong? No. It's just different. However, I do feel that if a scene is properly cut, it can play on its own. I know of several films that are dramatic and play very well with no music at all. *Executive Suite* has absolutely no music, but the actors and the drama enhanced by William Reynolds's editing carry the picture. With the exception of a few musical montages, *Butch Cassidy and the Sundance Kid* plays without music. With the right music and sound, anything can be made to look good—and that can fool you.

Editors are asked to do more. They are becoming editing auteurs in the work they do. It's neither good nor bad; it's just the way it is. Amen.

Chapter 35

The Death of Dailies

A few semesters ago David Rosenbloom was kind enough to address my editing class on the subject of *Black Mass*, a film he had edited that was currently playing. During the course of his talk I asked him about dailies. He turned to me with a wistful look and said, "I'm sorry, Jack. There are no more dailies. I haven't worked on a show with dailies in over two years."

I can't say that I was surprised, but I was saddened. In the brave new world of digital technology, we have lost a piece of filmmaking that was very important. The screening rooms where we gathered to evaluate the first efforts of our projects are no more. Dailies have always been the crucial moment when the future of a show can be changed.

Dailies, or rushes, as the English call them, are simply the days shooting synced up and usually presented in some sort of order. On *The Winds of War*, we ran the dailies three times. I would watch them in the morning with the studio executives. Then they would go to ABC for the executives to watch and then back to the studio where I would watch them with the director and crew.

I worked for a director named Robert E. Pearson who didn't want actors to ever see the dailies. He was afraid an actor would see his performance and then want to change it. Other directors I've worked for are happy to let actors view the dailies. Most actors don't seem to be that interested. Director Christian Nyby (*The Thing from Another World*) never watched dailies. He said, "I know what I shot. If there's a problem, it's not me."

Although I, like most editors, used to bitch about the time spent going to dailies, I feel it was important. Tom Rolf on *Heat* would often be in dailies for five hours due to the amount of footage being shot. I marveled that he had time to cut the picture. Seeing them particularly on the big screen gave you a real relationship to the material. I frequently walked out of dailies knowing exactly how I would put the scene together and what shots I would use.

Years ago when I was working for a low-budget company called PM Entertainment, I was asked by Shari Bowles, the head of production, about pickup shots. "When you were at MGM, how many pickups did you average per show?" she asked. "None," I replied. She was surprised and said that the editors on their television show *L.A. Heat* were spending five or six days shooting pickups. I told her, "You and the heads of post need to watch the dailies together."

When dailies came in at PM, the editor got a cassette to load into AVID, and the executives passed around a cassette that they individually watched. I knew they didn't have film dailies so I suggested they view the dailies on the largest possible television screen in the building. They began doing this, and shooting pickups began to vanish. During dailies, they could see what was missing and call the set to get it shot right away.

Many a time I have spotted things in dailies that have saved us. Beyond that, it is the best possible introduction to the material. When we were on film, we needed to watch the dailies if only to make sure we were in sync. Also, in watching them you are getting a message from the director by seeing what choices he made in covering a scene and what he felt was important. Often on *The Winds of War* Dan Curtis was half a world away from me, but he was speaking to me directly in the material he shot. Even without notes I could tell what was in his mind.

My fear with this current situation is that much of value is seeping through the cracks. It feels much different watching something on the screen as opposed to your cell phone or computer. The darkened screening room is a special place where our artistic juices can flow. It is almost a sacred place.

I fear as technology improves, we are moving too far to the technological side and neglecting our artistic side. Technology is only a tool, like a painter's brush. The brush does not determine the painting. The artist does. To take this farther, AVIDs do not edit movies; editors do. We are artists, and how the footage is presented to us has a large effect on how we deal with it. Viewing the dailies on the big screen—like God and DeMille intended—was never a waste of time.

Chapter 36   *The Passing of Film*

F ilm has been with us for more than 120 years in the making of movies. Now its days are numbered. Digital has gotten very good over the last few years. It's still not on par with film, however. High-def, as I write this, is up to about 8K in resolution. Film is 16K. It is the best medium of capture that there is. It has latitude, and there is more information in a frame of 35 mm film than in any frame of digital. Still, it is passing away. Why is that?

I remember when an episode of the hit series *Police Story* was shot on video back in the 1970s. It looked awful. It was a test, and all it proved was that you should shoot on film. But by the 1990s, digital was getting good, and high-def was coming out. Some television shows were being shot in high-def. Most, however, were still being captured on film and then converted to high-def for editing and finishing.

In 2008 the Screen Actors Guild's (SAG's) contract expired, and a strike was likely. It looked like we would not be having a television season. The American Federation of Television and Radio Artists (AFTRA), SAG's sister union, made an agreement with the Association of Motion Picture and Television Producers (AMPTP), but SAG held out. It looked like many people in the business besides actors would be thrown out of work if there were no season.

It was discovered that if a television show was not shot on film, it fell under the AFTRA contract and not the SAG contract. This meant that by not capturing on film, but on tape or digital, the season could go ahead. Many shows that been loyal to film started shooting in a different way. Now, SAG eventually settled, but the damage was done. Once they had done away with the cost of film, processing, and telecine, why go back?

Overnight the telecining of film dropped dramatically. It's interesting that 2008 was a big year for Deluxe Film Labs. Millions of feet of film were flowing in and out, and times were good. The lab had been the goose that laid the golden eggs that allowed Deluxe to acquire other companies and expand.

In the 1990s, places such as E Film in Hollywood had experimented with capturing film on a computer at high resolution. They were basically doing it for shots that needed a special effect or a computer-generated image (CGI). After that was done on a computer, the new shot could be recorded out to film and cut into the movie. The only problem was that this was expensive. It was $4 per frame going in and $4 per frame coming out. Now, when you consider that a frame is less than one twenty-fourth of a second, you can see where this is going. That's $96 per second each way.

Eventually, the price came down, and the concept of the digital intermediate (DI) was born. Traditionally, after a film finishes editing, negative is cut to match the edited work picture and a first trial answer print is struck. The lab's timer would adjust the colors and densities and make a print. After the first print, adjustments would be made and second print would be struck. Eventually, the print would be perfect.

After acceptance of the answer print, a timed interpositive would be made and from it internegatives to make the release prints for the theaters. This is where the labs made their real money: on a release print order of five thousand copies or more. This is also where film manufacturers such as Kodak and Fuji made their money.

The DI was a different way of dealing with finishing. Instead of cutting negative using the cut list, the negative could be scanned into the computer at high resolution. Once in there, it would be assembled to match your cut list. Then it would be color corrected in the computer. The beauty of this was that in a computer, portions of frames could be isolated and colored without affecting the rest of the frame. You could change the color of a man's shirt or change the color of leaves on trees to change the seasons.

Once accepted, the file created could be recorded back out to film to create a negative without a single splice in it. Release printing could be done from that. This had a number of advantages, including greater flexibility within the frame and not ever cutting the negative. This process became popular, along with a phrase on the set: "Don't worry. We'll fix it in the DI."

The studios were becoming very interested in digital projection. They liked the idea of not having to buy and ship 35 mm prints. A single print could easily run $2,000. Now, times that by five thousand, and you end up with $10,000,000. That's a sizeable piece of change. The theaters, on the other hand, weren't interested at all. They had their film projectors, and the system was working well for them. Why should they lay out money for new technology? The studios did not want to finance the theaters' converting, so why do it?

What changed everything was James Cameron's *Avatar*. This film was being released in a three-dimensional (3D) process that required going through a digital projector. In 3D the film had to be digital. Well, 3D had been languishing around for about sixty years on the back burner. Its time had come again. There was big money to be made in showing a film in 3D.

So, theaters began to convert, with some assistance from the studios. This meant that the days of the five thousand print orders were over. Now the film could play on a digital cinema package (DCP). It was a drive that the theaters could load onto a server with a special code and play the picture. It was much easier than six reels of film, and had nowhere near the shipping costs.

With the loss of print orders, the profit margins in labs dropped. One by one they began to close: CFI, Technicolor, and eventually Deluxe. In May 2014, Deluxe Film Labs closed its doors in Hollywood. That leaves Foto Kem as the only lab in Hollywood where you can get your negative processed, and how long the company will keep doing that is anybody's guess.

Fuji stopped making film at the end of 2013. Kodak had to reorganize by going through a bankruptcy.

There are still the die-hards: Christopher Nolan, Steven Spielberg, Quentin Tarantino, and various other filmmakers who favor film. They need a place to get their film processed. The bottom line will be whether a lab can still make a profit by processing film—or at least not take a loss.

Kodak feels there is still a future for its film products. They say that at least a third of filmmakers prefer to shoot on film. There are still one hundred film labs world wide and they feel they can still make a profit off negatives.

This also brings up the problem of preservation and archiving. Film, most notably in the form of YCMs, is the safest and most effective way to archive a motion picture. YCMs consist of the three basic colors—yellow, cyan, and magenta—which are printed to black-and-white panchromatic stock to preserve the color information. The silver halides of black and white do not fade like the vegetable dyes in color film do. Years later, the YCMs can be printed back together to create a new color negative.

Digital ways of preservation have been largely ineffective. Drives wear out, files lose their information, and who knows what will happen with the cloud? All of these methods require electronics to be working. If we were to see something happen to the power grid, all of this would vanish. In 1859 a coronal mass ejection from the sun struck the Earth, and for all intents and purposes wiped out the telegraphs in the United States and Europe. This was known as the "Carrington Event," and it is likely to happen again.

That aside, YCMs are still the safest way to preserve our films. Even if a picture is shot digitally, recording it out to black-and-white film is still the smart thing to do. But this does require a lab where film can be both processed and printed, and it further requires people who know how to do this. Hopefully, someone with authority understands this.

Chapter 37

The Red Camera, the Alexa, and Beyond

D igital cameras have become very sophisticated, and their prices have dropped. Arriflex, which for many years manufactured film cameras, has a very popular digital camera called the Alexa. When I was in the Air Force, Arriflex's film cameras were what we exclusively used for combat cameras. We filmed the Vietnam War with Arriflexes. The Alexa has been used on a number of studio films. In addition, Panavision, which was pretty much the standard for studio cameras, has developed its own digital camera.

The Red Camera has also become very popular in recent times, particularly because of its price. Starting at around $10,000, the camera is not entirely beyond the means of an individual. You can find cameramen who have their own Red Cameras. Several features have been shot using the Red Camera.

All of these cameras have a sensor that captures the information in the form of files. The files then, after being backed up, can be loaded into an editing system and completed. Then you can create a master file, which can be used to supply all of the requirements for distribution, from a DCP to a Blu-ray to a DVD.

As time passes, these cameras will no doubt improve and become the standards of the industry. For us in the editing room, the job will remain much the same: telling stories with pictures. Loading footage from tapes is fast disappearing as more and more things become file-based. Technology has encroached on us, but we have to live with it.

Originally, digital editing was sold on the idea that it would be faster—that we would save time. Actually, it has been just the opposite. The computers require more of us. Digital systems are making us go auteur. Now, when delivering a cut, particularly for television, we are expected to have cut sound effects, created CGIs, added a music score, added titles, and color-corrected the footage. With the Avid it is certainly possible to do all this, but it puts added pressure on the editor.

On film we would have had sound effects cut by a sound editor, music cut by a music editor, and a temp mix mixed in by a sound mixer. Now we are expected to do all of it. We are becoming jacks-of-all-trades. Our craft is changing, and we must change with it.

Several years ago, Steve Cohen, ACE, told me that computer editing would make everyone an editor. It has. When I was editing *Sherlock: Undercover Dog*, Richard Gardner asked me to show him how the EMC2 system worked. He was very computer literate, so I showed him. At night he would try cutting scenes in different ways from what I had done. Richard was smart, and he soon realized that he could not compete with me on that level.

On *Shannon's Rainbow*, the producer would try re-cutting the scenes that Patrea Patrick and I cut using Quick Time in Final Cut Pro. It didn't work that well, but occasionally we saw something worthwhile in the attempt. Many directors have gotten their own versions of Avid and use it to suggest how they think the scenes should go together.

The gods of time and space are under attack. In using the computer, we have totally demystified our craft, so that anyone is an editor. Well, maybe some are, but the real learning about editing comes from working under a skilled person. Democratizing editing was not a good idea, but we're stuck with it. It is our job to try to pass on to the next generation what we have learned about storytelling.

The times, they are a-changin'. I feel like the outlaws in Sam Peckinpah's epic *The Wild Bunch*. It was 1914, and they knew that they would have to look beyond their guns to survive. Now it's 2014, and I have changed with the times; I have learned to look beyond my guns and embrace the future, for better or worse. I am reminded of the line in the end of that movie spoken by Edmund O' Brien: "It ain't like the old days, but it'll do."

CPSIA information can be obtained
at www.ICGtesting.com
Printed in the USA
LVHW060946110219
607105LV00012B/544/P